GW01607451

JAMES TURRELL

LIGHTSCAPE

JAMES TURRELL

AT HOUGHTON HALL

LIGHTSCAPE SUPPORTERS

EXHIBITION SPONSORS
Christie's
Pace Gallery

FOUNDATION CIRCLE
Ivor Braka Ltd
Audemars Piguet
Coca-Cola Great Britain
Almine Rech Gallery and the Fundación Almine y Bernard Ruiz-Picasso para el Arte

PATRONS CIRCLE
Pierre Lagrange
François Gutzwiller
Dame Theresa Sackler DBE
Sybil Robson Orr
Mrs Chantal Miller

The publication is sponsored by Christie's

CHRISTIE'S

PACE

Published by Houghton Hall
on the occasion of the exhibition

LightSpace, James Turrell
June – October 2015

Houghton Hall
Norfolk PE31 8UE

Edited by David Cholmondeley
Copy-edited by Linda Schofield
Photography by Pete Huggins
Design and production by Peter Willberg
Colour reproductions by
Printmanagement Plitt

ISBN 978-0-9932882-0-3

Printed in Italy

CONTENTS

Foreword

When I was first introduced to James Turrell's work in the late 1990s, I was captivated by the contemplative, Zen-like quality of his light spaces. He seemed to be carrying the work of American painters from the previous generation, such as Mark Rothko, Barnett Newman and Ad Reinhardt into another dimension, as well as another medium. At the time, I was considering the introduction of contemporary works of art into the landscape around Houghton, and I invited him to come up with an idea for one of his iconic Skyspaces within the newly restored formal planting in front of the house, where areas of 'wilderness' were enclosed by a geometric design of beech hedges.

An old estate map from the 1720s, when Sir Robert Walpole was planning his new Palladian 'powerhouse', showed various small garden structures within this part of the grounds. They may have been temples, gazebos or fountains, but certainly focal points in a typically intricate scheme. They had long since disappeared and it seemed somehow appropriate to reinterpret the idea, adding something of our own time within a historic framework. Indeed it was the evidence of these earlier features that persuaded the planning authorities to allow us to proceed. The Skyspace became a sort of Modernist folly among the trees, but very much in the spirit of Walpole's grand design, delighting and surprising any visitor to the 'pleasure grounds', as the gardens at Houghton were once known.

Around the same time, we also acquired one of Turrell's interior Space Division pieces, *St Elmo's Breath* (1992), which had been included in his retrospective at the Museum of Applied Arts (MAK) in Vienna. There was no suitable room within the house itself, so we decided to use the eighteenth-century water tower in the park, which was originally designed by one of Sir Robert's friends, Henry, Earl of Pembroke. The ground floor – which had housed the iron water tank – was the ideal size for this haunting light piece that requires the viewer to acclimatise to the relative darkness to be seen properly.

I believe no one who has visited Turrell's Roden Crater project in Arizona can doubt his remarkable achievement as an artist. Yet his smaller pieces are also 'worlds in themselves' and part of the same extraordinary vision: works of exquisite purity and beauty that spring from his single-minded investigation into how we see and apprehend light and colour. These spaces are often austere and minimalist in form, yet can nevertheless provoke an intense response; the effect on the eye – and therefore on the mind – is sometimes only fully apparent after prolonged immersion in their ethereal atmosphere.

Unlike so much art produced today, Turrell's light spaces do not necessarily require specific knowledge or explanation to make their full impact, and can be readily appreciated by those who have little interest in abstraction or in 'contemporary art'; after all, light can affect us with an almost visceral immediacy. This is perhaps why they are popular with children and adults alike.

It has been a hugely rewarding experience, as well as a great privilege, to work with James Turrell on the two large-scale light installations at Houghton, and now to be able to present a major show of his work, with pieces that span almost the whole of his career, from the Projections of the 1960s to his recent series of holograms and Tall Glasses. We are also extremely proud that he will be creating a special illumination of the façade of the house: a spectacular display that will be open to visitors until late in the evening. I am enormously grateful to James for his open-handed commitment and enthusiastic involvement with the show, as well as to his wife, Kyung Lee Turrell, for her unfailing support.

Credit is also due to lighting technician Ryan Pike, and the many individuals and companies who have helped to set up the installations; also to Julia Triebes of the Turrell Studio for her assistance both in arranging the exhibition and compiling the catalogue. In the UK, Peter Wilson, Erica Bolton and Johnny Cornwell have all provided invaluable advice over many months.

LightScape has been a major undertaking for Houghton, and we would like to acknowledge the generous funding of exhibition sponsors Christie's and Pace Gallery, as well as members of our Foundation and Patrons Circles. We are also very much indebted to those who have lent works to the show.

For the catalogue, I would especially like to thank Peter Murray CBE, founder and director of the Yorkshire Sculpture Park (home to another Skyspace), for his essay on James Turrell, and Hiram C. Butler, gallerist and professor at Rice University, Houston, for engaging in a fascinating dialogue with the artist; also Peter Willberg, who has designed a book of great elegance, and Pete Huggins, who has embellished it with some beautiful photographs.

Finally my heartfelt gratitude to our remarkable team at Houghton, and to my wife, Rose, who have all worked tirelessly on preparations for *LightScape*. I hope visitors will enjoy seeing Houghton from a very different perspective, and will be as intrigued and elated by Turrell's light works as I was when I first saw them.

David Cholmondeley

Greeting the Light

He started life as a Quaker, stopped for a time and then went back to it. He gained his pilot's licence at 16 and has logged thousands of hours of flying time, including runs in single-engine planes across the Himalayas to help evacuate monks from Tibet during the aftermath of the 1959 rebellion. He spent time in jail as a conscientious objector. He studied perceptual psychology before art. He purchased land with a defunct volcano in Arizona and started a cattle ranch. From this fascinating and varied background James Turrell has emerged as one of the most awe-inspiring artists of his generation. He makes extraordinary art and has established an international reputation creating major site-specific works in 22 countries and in 14 of the 50 United States of America, his home country.

The dramatic and unprecedented speed of change during the twentieth century was reflected in creative practices and in terms of the concept, meaning and definition of art. Its boundaries were detonated, which art critic Robert Hughes (1938–2012) described in the title of his memorable 1980s television documentary series as 'the shock of the new'. The search for the new is generally accepted to be an important ingredient of contemporary art. Although this would seem to be an essential component of Turrell's innovative approach to art, as the writer Lily Van Ginneken observed, 'he is not actually engaged in creating something new. It is more about creating conditions that allow viewers to see and experience what light is and what it does to space'.[1] Dematerialisation is essential to Turrell's work; it is concerned with the shaping of visual experiences. Through his art, he hopes viewers, as 'co-creators', might recognise that 'they are part of creating that which we think we perceive'. For Turrell 'there is no object, no image and no focus, what are you looking at? You are looking at the looking'. When asked what you own when you purchase one of his works, Turrell is reputed to have replied, 'you own the light passing through it'.

Light is everything to Turrell. For him there is a truth in light; it is something that exists only by burning material. Essential to survival, it is for many also equated with religious or spiritual experiences. When he was a child, Turrell's grandmother often recalled that 'as you sat in Quaker silence you were able to go inside to greet the light'. The concept of greeting the light left an indelible mark on the artist's thinking, his fascination with light and spirituality: 'My art deals with light itself not as a bearer of revelation but as revelation itself'.

Graduate studies in psychology shifted to the study of art at the University of California and in 1969 he participated in the Art and Technology project organised by the Los Angeles County Museum of Art. His initial experiments with light started prior to this when, in 1966, he made his first light projections during his rental of the Mendota Hotel, when he covered the windows so allowing only prescribed amounts of daylight into the building.

Turrell's Skyspaces started to evolve in the 1970s. The concept is very simple: an enclosed space is punctured by an aperture in the roof to the sky. Over the years he has refined this idea through a series of mesmerising spaces in many parts of the world, from Houston, Texas to Houghton, Norfolk.

I first met James Turrell in 1993 when he was working with Director Robert Hopper (1946–99) at the now long-gone Henry Moore Sculpture Trust Studio at Dean Clough in Halifax. During that period he spent much time at the Yorkshire Sculpture Park (YSP) walking through the landscape and examining the history and details of the Bretton estate. He was drawn to a dilapidated deer shelter, an eighteenth-century functional folly, built into the landscape to protect the herd that at one time roamed the parkland. From this encounter he developed a plan to turn the shelter into a Skyspace. It took over a decade, and the crucial support of the Art Fund, to raise the money and transform what Andrew Graham-Dixon has described as an historic structure, a shelter for deer, into a refuge for people. The contrast between the rustic build and the Quaker minimalism of the interior provides a cultural overlay as one sits and absorbs the sound of the wind, the passage of time and the changing light qualities from above: 'The beautiful thing in Yorkshire is the wonderful maritime skies. You realise that England is at sea, and this beautiful cloudscape, the greyness of it, was something spectacular to me, and also the fact that I could finally take this sky and give it the blue which is its due.'[2]

It is very likely that Turrell was even more aware of the maritime skies and 'that England is at sea' when he first visited Houghton Hall, around 12 miles from the Norfolk coast. He has a great love of English history and landscape, both of which he found in abundance at Houghton when he made his first visit in August 1999.

Houghton Hall was built for Sir Robert Walpole (1676–1745) in 1735 as an expression of the power, privilege and prestige of Britain's first Prime Minister. The result is one of the finest examples of Palladian architecture ever constructed. The exquisitely proportioned house is surrounded by over 1,000 acres of designed landscape. The soft planes of the gentle, green Norfolk land complement the

grand, but refined, silver-white of the stone buildings. Tapping into the history and the gentle vertical and horizontal nature of the Houghton estate, Turrell created two major site-specific works: *Seldom Seen* (2002) and *St Elmo's Breath* (1992). The latter, a brilliant concept linking past and present, is housed inside Walpole's water tower, which was built as a working folly in 1731 before the hall was completed; functional follies, as we have found at YSP, have a great attraction for Turrell.

St Elmo's Breath is a Turrell Space Division, a large and open light-emitting aperture cut horizontally into an interior wall, creating a new existence for this oddly proportioned, quirky Palladian water tower beautifully located against the vast skies of Norfolk.

Seldom Seen was designed and built by Turrell for Houghton. This twenty-first-century folly, an oak-clad Skyspace constructed on stilts, is located in a more secluded garden area of the park. Hedges of hornbeam plot the route to a pathway outlined by curved box hedges, leading visitors up a gently raised walkway to views of the park from a balcony that contains the entrance to the inner chamber of *Seldom Seen*. Although each of the numerous Skyspaces Turrell has created in different parts of the world has its own character and identity, generally speaking they are single, specifically proportioned rooms designed to house around 15 to 20 people with an aperture cut into the roof opening to the sky. At YSP the organic nature of the *Deer Shelter* exterior suits the slightly rough terrain edging towards the Pennines, the backbone of England. It provides a contrast with the more elegant formality of *Seldom Seen*, nestling in the tranquil setting of Houghton. Whatever the style or shape of aperture the aim is to bring the viewer nearer to the sky, encouraging contemplation, heightening their sense of perceiving light and space. For Turrell, perception is the object.

Turrell has sometimes been described as a land artist and he certainly, along with his fellow American artist Michael Heizer (b.1944) and others, blurs the boundaries between object, experience and content. As for Robert Smithson (1938–1973), the creator of the *Spiral Jetty* (1970) at the Great Salt Lake in Utah, the aeroplane became an extension of Turrell's practice. Flying above the earth offers an opportunity to see space differently: not physical but atmospheric. From his cockpit 'light is immaterial and this shapes the space'. As Turrell criss-crossed the vastness of the American South-west in his plane he eventually discovered Roden Crater. There, in the Painted Desert of Arizona, the artist is creating a masterpiece, a life's work and one of the greatest statements of contemporary art. This unimaginably ambitious piece of land art, monumental in scale and thought, continues to transform a lifeless, 390,000-year-old volcano into a series of Chambers, Skyspaces and experiences aligned to celestial events for the next 12,000 years. According to Turrell, more astronomical events have been witnessed from this area of Arizona than from any other part of the world. Although Roden Crater has become the core of Turrell's artistic existence, it also feeds his concern with exhibiting in different parts of the world and stimulates his natural curiosity to develop new projects in varied locations.

Houghton Hall, which could not be in greater contrast to the Painted Desert, is a case in point and having worked on two site-specific projects in this serene corner of Norfolk it seems fitting that Houghton, under the direction of David Cholmondeley, presents a rare opportunity to experience a new Turrell exhibition: *LightScape*. Various installations will transform the visual appearance of the historic architecture. This bold initiative coincides with UNESCO's 2015 International Year of Light, to celebrate light and its essential importance for the existence of life itself, as well as the impact of photonics on the world. *LightScape* offers not only the chance to see major works but also an insight into Turrell's practice through a series of models, made in 2008, of aspects of Roden Crater including *Crater's Eye*, along with a beautiful display of 20 etchings from the First Light series made between 1989 and 1990. More recent holograms and a piece from the Tall Glass series (2015) afford a link with the re-creation of impressive projection works from 1968, which established light as the artist's primary medium. The combination of drawings, photographs and film in this exhibition bring together over 47 years of creativity, providing a compelling statement of Turrell's innovative work.

The two projection pieces originally conceived in 1968, *Raethro, Red* and *Enzu, Green*, are made by focusing a single controlled beam of light from the corner of a room to create an apparently three-dimensional object and perceptual substance: a bright red pyramid in *Raethro, Red* and a green plane of light connecting floor to ceiling in *Enzu, Green*. These works investigate the way in which light can be given volume and spatiality in a room through their interaction with viewers.

Closely related to the projection pieces are Turrell's holograms. At Houghton Hall a transmission hologram and three small holograms, from 2008–10, are part of the exhibition. His holograms are not attempts to create the illusion of objects by using light. Although he employs holograms to examine their phenomena, light itself becomes the object. Like the projection pieces, they thus examine the physicality and mass of light, allowing it to become the object of the viewing.

More akin to the title of the exhibition, *LightScape*, are the works from the Tall Glass series, which consist of an aperture covered with frosted glass, behind which are LEDs or neon lights, programmed to change colour slowly over a period of time.

One of the unique features of the exhibition is the site-specific illumination of the entire magnificent western façade of Houghton Hall. The relationship between interior and exterior light has always fascinated Turrell, as has the link between natural and artificial light and architecture. After initial architectural light works made in Germany and Japan in 1997, Turrell progressed towards a series of lit building projects throughout 2000. They ranged from the historic to the modern, and from commercial spaces to museums, including *MAKlight* (2004), Museum of Applied Arts, Vienna, Austria; *Four Eyes* (2007), Kunsthalle Mannheim, Germany; *Night Flight* (2009), Dornier Aviation Museum, Friedrichshafen, Germany; and *Light Raiment II* (2008), Franklin Park Conservatory, Columbus, Ohio, USA. Although most were illuminated from within, some, like Houghton Hall, were lit from outside.

At Houghton, Turrell's architectural light project links the colonnades, the arched loggias in the exterior wings, the towers and the impressive cupolas. The soft daylight of Norfolk complements the gentle, subtle nature and artificial light gradations of a slowly changing illumination programme, which appears to reach its zenith around dusk and on into the night. This remarkable and beautiful piece of Palladian architecture finds a new transitory existence as a striking spectacle of light and space.

In the hands of Turrell the delicate choreography required to merge history and state of the art technology creates a continuity between past and present and it not only links the central part of Houghton Hall with its wings but also history and science, providing viewers with an unusual perceptual encounter. The dematerialisation of the object through illumination prompts viewers as 'co-creators' to perceive the building afresh and see it, literally, in a different light as Turrell continues to examine the limits and marvels of visual perception. The illumination of Houghton Hall is a wonderful and sensuous achievement and is a rare opportunity to see a new major James Turrell exhibition in Britain.

Despite the technologies and intricate planning behind Turrell's projects, it is worth reflecting on what the New York art critic Calvin Tomkins said about the artist: 'his work is not about light or a record of light: it is light'.[3] This emphasises once more Turrell's belief that 'my art deals with light itself not as the bearer of revelation, but as revelation itself'.

Turrell always wants to provide us with an opportunity to reflect, to absorb the processes and engage with his projects. In this fast-paced world his work encourages 'the joy of sensing and the sensual' expanding what he has described as wordless thought. The great American artist Chuck Close said that James Turrell is an 'orchestrator of experience, not a creator of cheap effects. And every artist knows how cheap an effect is, and how revolutionary an experience'.[4]

Peter Murray

1 Turrell, James, Lily Van Ginneken, Gerrit Willems et al., *James Turrell: Hemels Gewelf in Kijkduin / Celestial Vault in the Dunes*. The Hague: Stroom Den Hague Centre for Visual Arts, 1996.
2 James Turrell quoted in *The Deer Shelter*, Illuminations film, 2006.
3 Calvin Tomkins, 'Flying into the Light', *The New Yorker*, vol. 78, issue 42 (13 January 2003), p. 1.
4 *New York Times Magazine*, 16 June 2013.

Interview

HIRAM C. BUTLER: I was surprised when I heard that you were going to have an exhibition at Houghton Hall, with its extraordinary eighteenth-century architecture and collections of Old Masters and antiquities. I knew about it through the recent exhibition at the Museum of Fine Arts in Houston [*Houghton, Portrait of an English Country House*, MFAH, June – September 2014]. I met David and Rose and we went and looked at your piece [at Rice University, Houston], and I thought, 'Wow, how are they going to show James's work?' How did you feel about showing at Houghton Hall?

JAMES TURRELL: Well, first of all, there's work that's permanently installed there, a Skyspace that's in the garden, raised up to the level of the trees, and then … in the folly that was the water tank for the house, now supplanted by another water system, I installed *St Elmo's Breath* (1992), a Space Division piece, or aperture work. They also have a couple of Projections, a Tall Glass, a large hologram and quite a few prints. So David has been collecting and has been doing very well with it. I'll have a show of some work that he's selected of mine. So, in that way it feels very appropriate.

HB: It's a continuation of what Sir Robert Walpole started.

JT: That's correct.

HB: Except that … some of the work that he collected and certainly the architecture of the time were contemporary.

JT: Oh yes, it was all done when it was being made.

HB: So … David is doing the same thing around 300 years later.

JT: And it's hopeful that the house can be kept, but who knows how these things go because new governments and taxes make these places difficult to hang on to.

HB: It was interesting to find out about David's management and the land usage because to maintain the art he's doing much of what you're doing to conserve Roden Crater [in Arizona] in terms of …

JT: … maintaining the land around it, yes.

HB: Yes, the land around it. He has organic farming and livestock and you're doing the same thing.

JT: Yes.

HB: That was a great surprise to me.

JT: I don't quite have the manor house, yet, you realise.

[laughter]

HB: No, ... but you've got the equivalent of a 35-storey building underground that you have to maintain.

JT: Yes, that's true.

HB: They're sort of equal responsibilities. ... I'm obsessed with antiquities and I was reading about the poetry of Lucretius and how he combined philosophy and physics ... I think in many ways what you do is combining ... his writing is in the form of poems, so it's art ... and your work is a combination of physics and art.

JT: Well, no. The technology comes from physics. The art is not really anything to do with physics. I often keep it separate because this work is not about science ... it doesn't inform science at all. So it's not science.

HB: It's employing the technology and you're using that.

JT: Yes, but that's no different from painters today going down to the art shop where they can buy hundreds, literally hundreds, of premixed paints. So you don't need to be a chemist or an alchemist to really have good quality paint. You were on the edge of that in the Renaissance, I mean, they were often very secretive about how they got their paints and jealously guarded their own formulations. But now, that's not true for painting.

But, for light it's been very difficult. I had to start out with neon and filters and all sorts of things to get the colours I wanted. And now you can do that so easily with the technology of, firstly, the LED, which has changed remarkably in the last ten years, and, secondly, the computer programs that can run these lights in very sophisticated and multi-fixtured arrays. You can really control the light very beautifully. I hoped to do that when I was young and tried to do it with all manner of equipment but it was, sort of, *deus ex machina*: I had to hide the physical machinery of the large transformers. We can make that tunnel [at MFAH] so much more easily today with LED lights than I did with the neon light.

HB: The transitions of the light and colour in the beginning were all made using sunrise and sunset and now you can use other forms of light.

JT: Oh, yes ... in those early pieces I would let the transition be with the light outside, and the light inside stayed the same. That was all with tungsten light. That's the very simplest way to do it. Those were the early Skyspaces, like at PS1 [New York], or the one that's owned by the Einsteins [art collectors Cliff and Mandy Einstein] in Brentwood [California].

HB: Something that really struck me is that at the Quaker Meeting House in Houston, after the sun has set and you close the roof on the Skyspace and then you turn on the second, blue light piece, and you walk back into the Meeting room ... the light seems to contain particles. I'm always taken by the atomic nature that you give to light.

JT: That's quite illusory because we don't, of course, see atoms. But there is this graininess that comes ... and in the pieces of the Danaë series of the Space Division works, that's when light is on both sides of the aperture, you can get this very interesting quality where it looks as though there's a grain to the light. There's a finer grain to the blue and a thicker grain to the red end of the spectrum, so you can see this quality of light existing in the air that is, sort of, corpuscular, or as you say, atomic. But anyway, it's a graininess that comes from how we see. It's not how the light is; it's how our vision is. That quality, of giving light a physical presence in the air, is something I like very much, ... when you look into it, it's as if you're looking through some *thing* to see the wall that's actually there. And this is light inhabiting the space as opposed to just being on the wall.

HB: I feel like I'm walking through the light.

JT: Well you are in many pieces, like the Ganzfeld pieces where you go up the steps and are then inserted into what would be *like* a Space Division. You know, there were people that would dive through the aperture thinking it was going to be soft inside ... and several were injured. That happened at the Whitney in New York, and also at the Whitney a woman leaned against what she thought was a wall and just fell backwards.

HB: I watched school children go through the tunnel and they reached out, trying to touch the light. They felt that it was actually a surface there.

JT: It is. ... there is light there but the fact that I make it feel like a surface is another matter and it makes people want to touch it. But I like that because I think that we do touch light and it's very much a feeling sense, particularly when you lower the light levels and the pupil opens ... so that feeling goes out of the eye like touch. And then I think we really feel things. A lot of people attribute a romantic quality to it because it's often under lowered light that we make love or are involved with another individual in that way ... like when you go to a restaurant and they have the regular lighting, and then somewhere around 5:30 or 6 ... boom ... the lights start to turn down.

HB: Right.

JT: They usually put candles on the table and sometimes you can't even read the menu ... [laughter] It really is true, we feel light more in those circumstances and it's something that's a very lovely sense to have. So all those things work in the favour of art. And there are some writings by Leonardo da Vinci where he likes to have the art come out of the gloaming, as he calls it.

HB: Yes.

JT: That is, when the light is very low and you don't even necessarily see the framing of the work, you just see this image kind of coming out of the darkness. And he liked that very much. That's something where we're really feeling ... the act of seeing is an act of feeling. And I think that's very important. It has been said about my work, 'well, you call yourself a light artist but you use precious little of it'.

[laughter]

HB: If light is both a wave and a particle …

JT: It's only a particle. It is a photon and a photon has mass. So it is only a particle. Light is a physical thing. It is matter converted into energy. And so it does exhibit wave phenomena, just like water does. Water is a physical substance, as is light. … And there is wave phenomena …, in fact there are phenomena that can pass over the wave front … I mean, phenomena that can travel faster than the speed that light itself is travelling. That's no different from, say, a tsunami that goes faster than water. The water doesn't move. The water is going up and down, and these phenomena go through it, through the medium. So, that's one of the things about light … It's very good to read the book by Richard Feynman called QED. It stands for 'quantum electrodynamics', but QED is also what you put after a mathematical proof is accomplished and it means, 'thus it is proven' in Latin. Feynman was a terrible punster, and [laughter] … he received the Nobel Prize in physics [in 1965] and worked on the atomic bomb [during the Second World War], for which he was forever sorry … but it was an interesting matter to really understand light. I mean, … the skin absorbs it and then we create vitamin D from this exposure to light. So light is actually a food and we deal with it physically as a food and it's very much a part of our diet.

HB: Do you employ wave phenomena in your work?

JT: Not really, not any more than superficially. I do work with polarised light. I polarise the light in different directions across the seeming … wall of light that curtails the space in the Wedgework pieces.

There, across the wave front, I'm actually polarising light. … it helps you to see this … greater thickness, or the stopping of one volume of light by another volume of light. I always wanted to make an architecture of light, and that happens during the day when the sun lights the atmosphere and you can't see through it anymore. So then we have this idea of sky …

HB: Right.

JT: When the light no longer lights the atmosphere, as at night, you see through it to the universe. This change of space is dramatic but we're not wonderfully familiar with the universe because of the lighting of cities.

HB: It's remarkable how that confines our space.

JT: It is how we were able to pass the dark skies ordinance in Flagstaff [Arizona]. The Indians proposed it and they were very concerned by the fact that when you light the atmosphere you can't see through the sky anymore, as in the day … that doing that at night was then lessening the territory we inhabit. We were essentially made less by this spillage of night-light that we employ because of our fear. We sort of want to take the daytime existence all the way into night… . But that reduces the territory we visually inhabit. I always felt that you needed to at least see the Milky Way, … its two spiral arms … and we're about two-thirds out on one of those arms. So, it's very interesting to make that as the measure, … the amount of space that we inhabit with our consciousness. And I've looked at the pieces I do in the way that you look into space, and sometimes you are in it as well. … certainly with the Ganzfeld pieces and some of the more involved art spaces … I've always wanted to have an architecture of light.

HB: I've only experienced that in art twice. The first time was when I walked into the Rothko Chapel and I felt as if I was both in a work of art and looking at a work of art, and the space in those paintings was limitless. The second time was when I saw your piece at the Capp Street …

JT: Capp Street Project [in San Francisco].

HB: … in 1983. I had that same sensation that I was both in the work of art and I was looking at the work of art.

JT: It's one of the reasons I've always liked the Ganzfeld series where you see this, essentially an aperture work … but you look up and see a plane of light with steps up to it.

HB: Now … there's something that has been a part of everyone's conversation … and that's people involving themselves physically in your retrospective at the National Gallery of Australia in Canberra, by walking through your pieces nude.

JT: Well, I had first noticed it in Japan, for the Gasworks piece, which is a sphere that you are pushed into on a sort of morgue slab, so that your eye is at the centre of the sphere. In Japan they bought all of these small works that you can get inside and are essentially for one person at a time. In Kanazawa they have the first of the Gasworks that I actually made and they seemed to like those works. I found out they had this little thing where you went in and you took your clothes off and put a yukata on, which is a type of cotton kimono for the bath. They would very demurely climb into the piece, lie down, get pushed in and then they open it to the light. Particularly in the solar plexus and on the chest you feel the light literally bombarding you. It's quite interesting. I mentioned this in Australia because they [National Gallery, Canberra] purchased a piece called *Bindu Shards*.

HB: Is that a Gasworks piece?

JT: It's a Gasworks-style sphere. A Meditation Space is what we call them now. Anyway, I mentioned this and it was talked around. They have an artist who leads nude tours of art and so they signed him up and he led a tour of my exhibition. Apparently it was a media sensation. [laughter] I was criticised very much in the *Guardian* by the art critic who had reviewed my work positively before. I do think it's important to expose yourself to art and to expose yourself to light. It's healthful. It's a healthy activity. This made people go every which way, as you can imagine. People were joyously celebrating the fact that they could go into a national gallery without any clothes on. People would arrive there, go to the bathroom, take their clothes off; it was pretty wild.*

* At Canberra three after-hours tours were offered to a limited number of participants who signed up for them.

[laughter]

HB: I can't tell you how remarkable that is to me, because I know people that will not enter a museum unless they're in a coat and tie!

JT: Absolutely. Well, even a bow tie.

HB: Exactly.

[laughter]

JT: And I'm talking to one.

[laughter]

JT: The Director, Gerard [Folliott Vaughan], said, oh well, I'm not doing this, but please go ahead. See, we are unable to stop this now.

[laughter]

HB: I'm hopping around here ... but you told me, or perhaps I read it somewhere, that all of the information that we get about the universe is carried by light.

JT: Yes. There is content in light. That is, we can tell what a star is made of from the spectrum of light it gives off. And we can tell, not only what the materials are that are burning, but the temperature at which they are burning, and we can also tell how fast the star is receding from us. There are very, very few stars that are coming towards us. Everything is going away from us. It's very interesting, the expansion of the universe that is happening. And so this is how we can know a star without touching it.

HB: Then I remember you talking about how red light from the furthest reaches of the universe comes to us and it's billions of years old ...

JT: It's not so much red light, but the spectrum is red shifted. Shifted towards the red. The whole spectrum is shifted towards the red. It comes from that star.

HB: ... and it knows that we're seeing it.

JT: Well, light knows when we're looking. It exhibits a different behaviour, which is very bizarre, and Arthur Zajonc and a number of other physicists have been involved in these experiments. Generally, we use light to illuminate other things. My interest, of course, is in the 'thingness' of light: its physicality and the presence, the felt presence, of light in the space that we enter consciously by looking into it. Generally, we don't look at light; we just look at the thing that is illuminated by the light. We're sort of using this light in almost a slave-master manner rather than actually letting it speak for itself. I'm interested in the revelation of the light itself rather than that which it illuminates. It's in this chain of how art has developed over time ... consider the work of other artists, whether it's Constable or Turner, whether it's Vermeer with a more intellectual light, or Velázquez or Goya with a very emotional light. Then all of the Impressionists as well, not to mention Rothko and, of course, one of my favourites,

Ad Reinhardt, who has light come out of darkness. Beautiful, lush colour coming out of darkness.

HB: Wow. I'd never thought of that before, but the Capp Street Project was like looking at a Reinhardt.

JT: Yes. Very much so.

HB: Yeah!

JT: So, that quality, even when seeing it in some of the Skyspaces when the ceiling disappears … you try to chase that colour, because you look at this colour with Reinhardt and you can see it … and then it sort of goes funny. You're pursuing it but not getting there. It's something that I've found really beautiful in Reinhardt's work, and he's a great artist. He approached the sublime in a very disciplined manner. Rothko was more haphazard … occasionally a bit …

HB: Romantic?

JT: Yes, he was hit and miss, but Reinhardt would just stay right on it and not let it go. I found that very, very remarkable. These are all my heroes and they're all working with light, although they're doing it with paint, so I just wanted to actually use light itself.

Façade Illumination, Houghton Hall, 2015

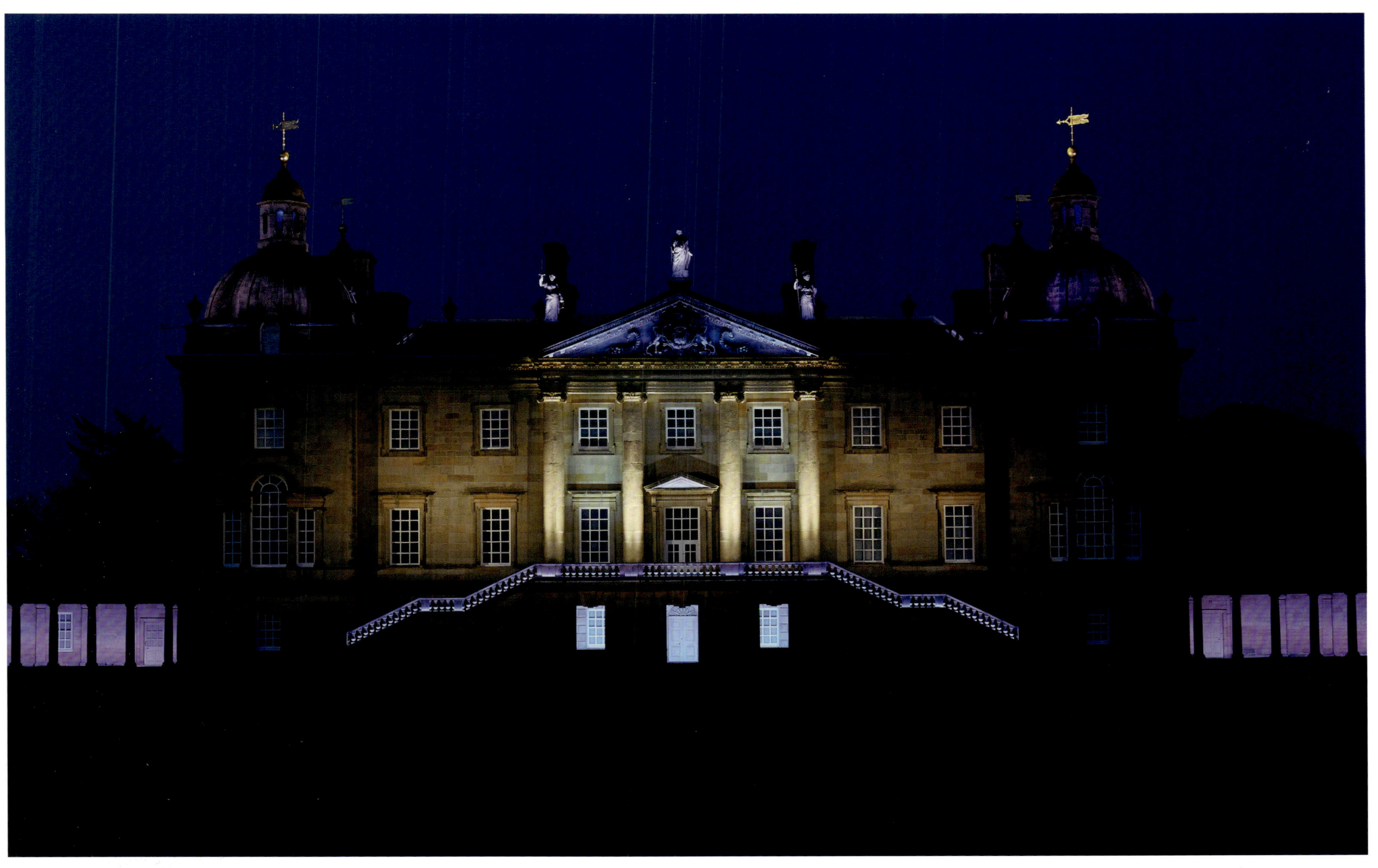

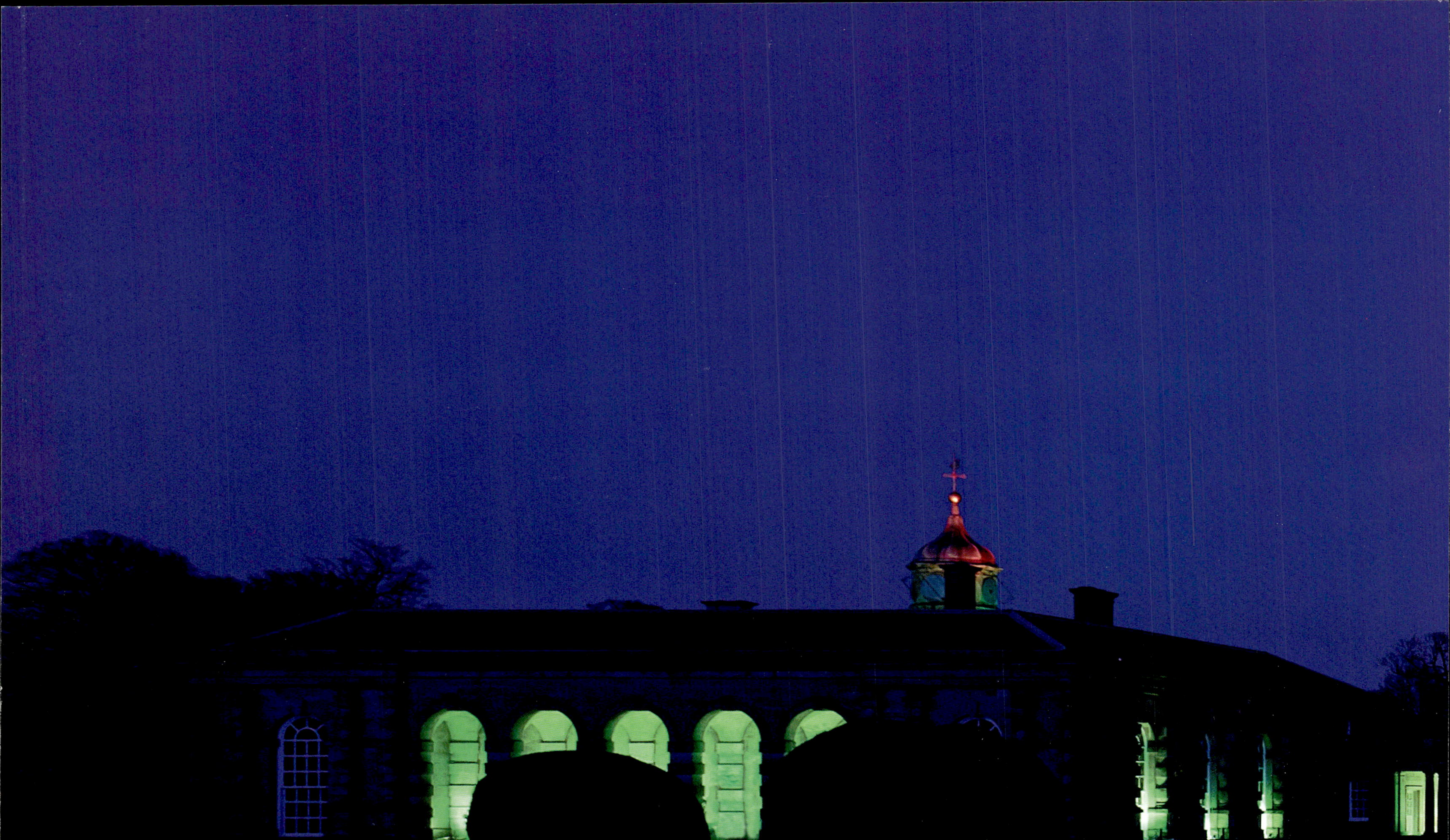

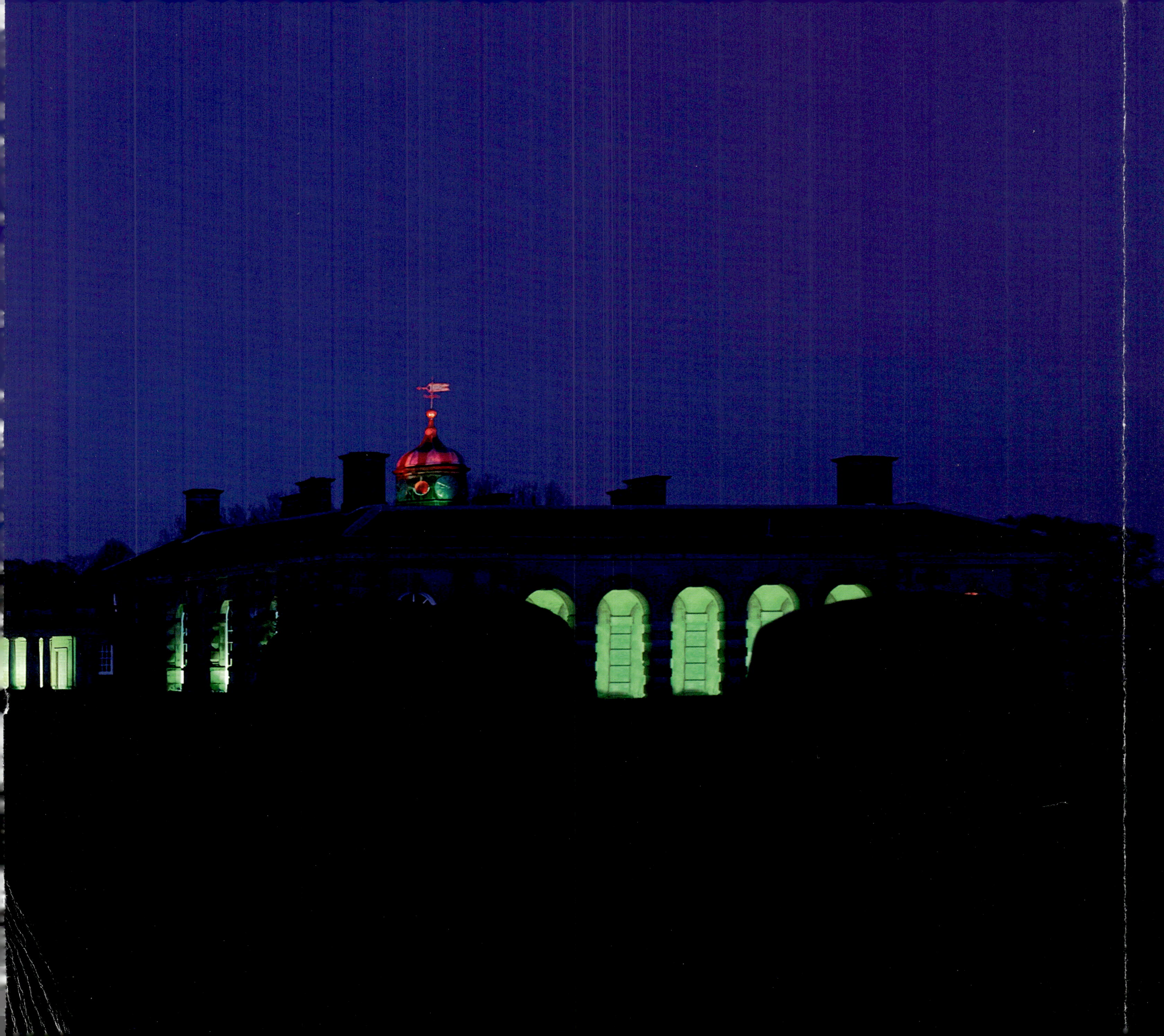

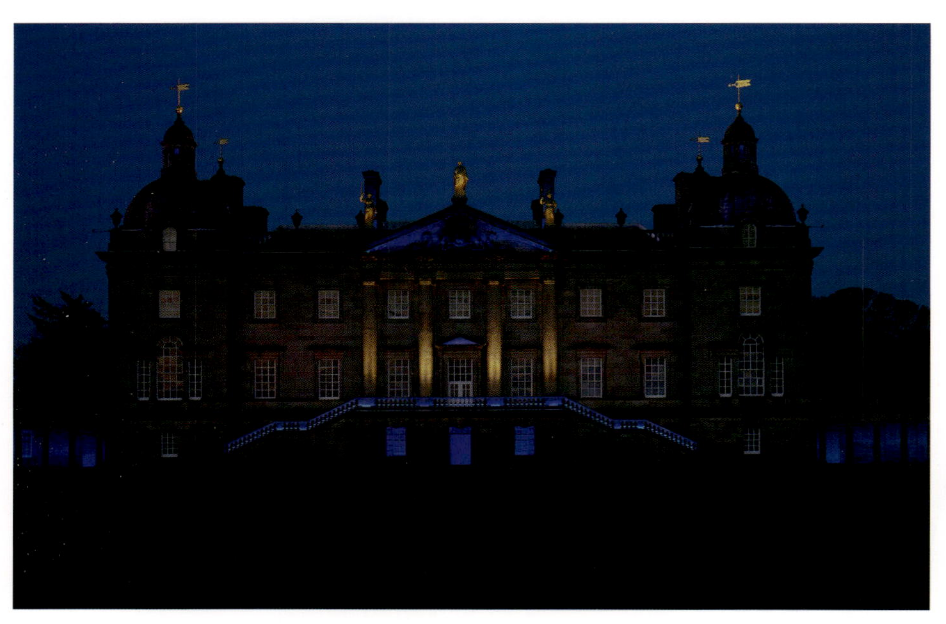

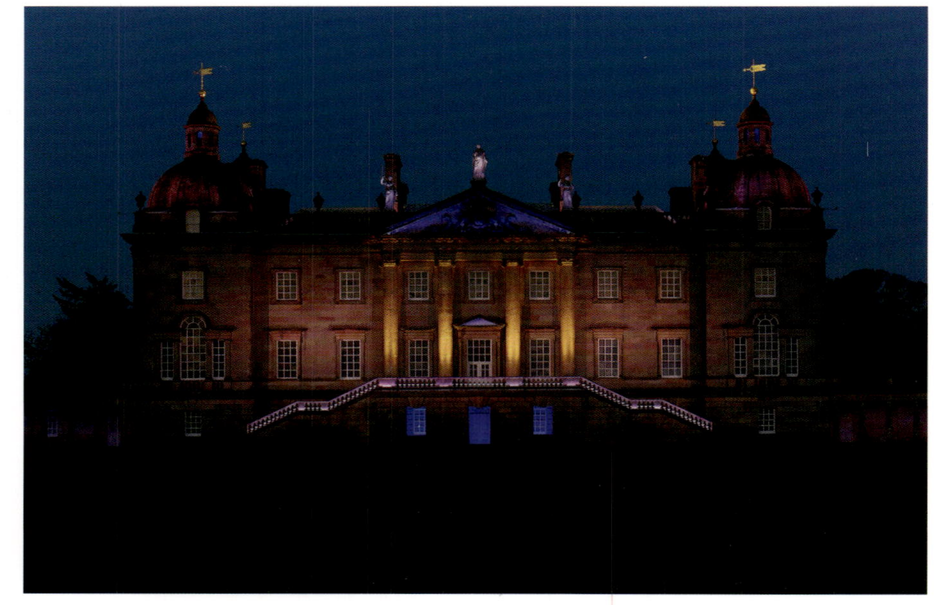

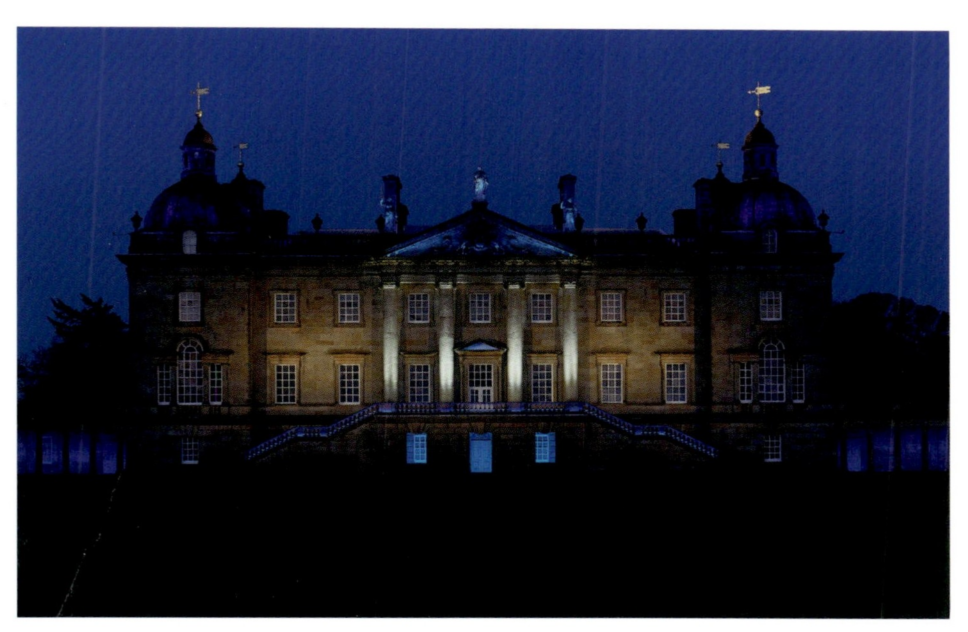

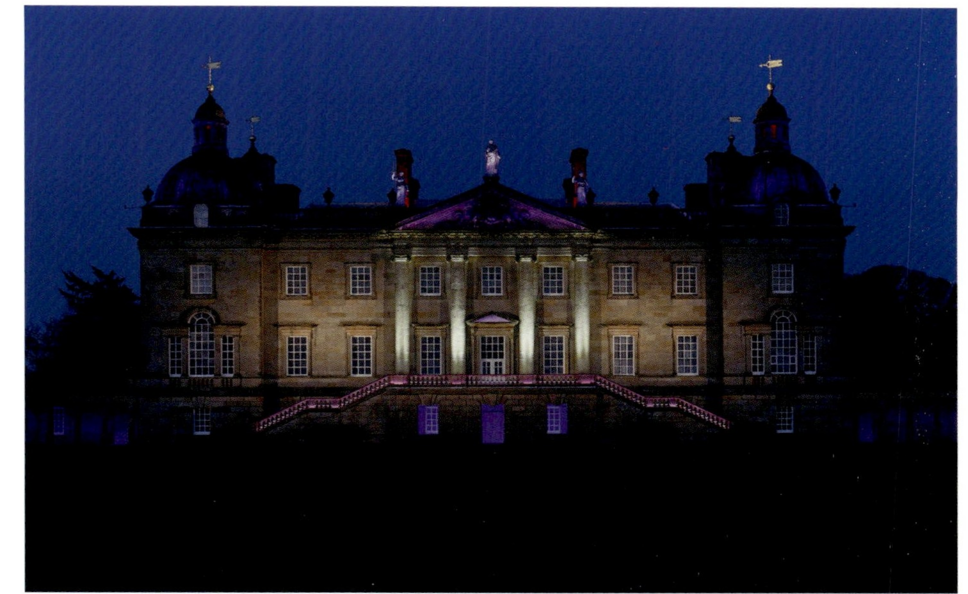

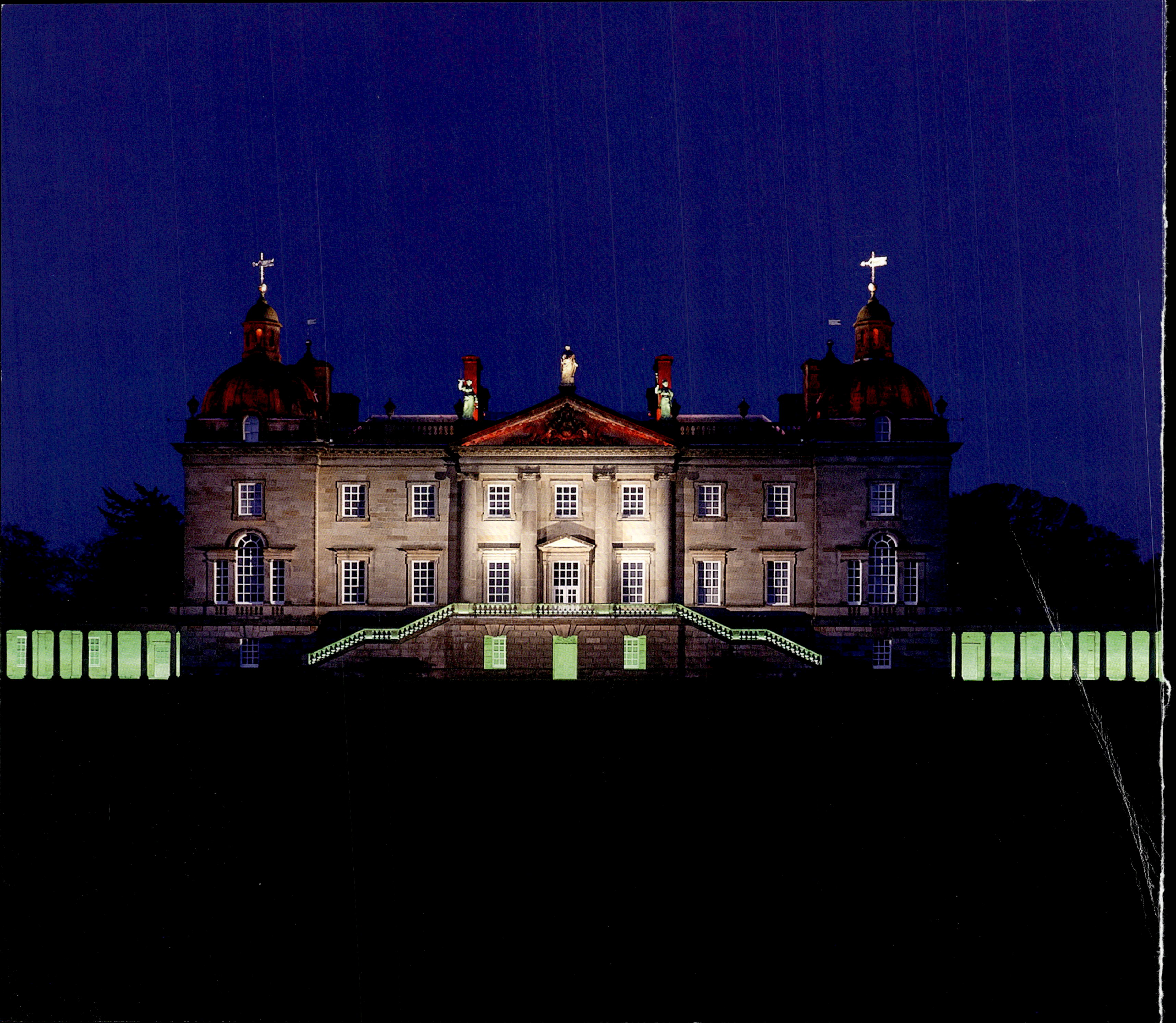

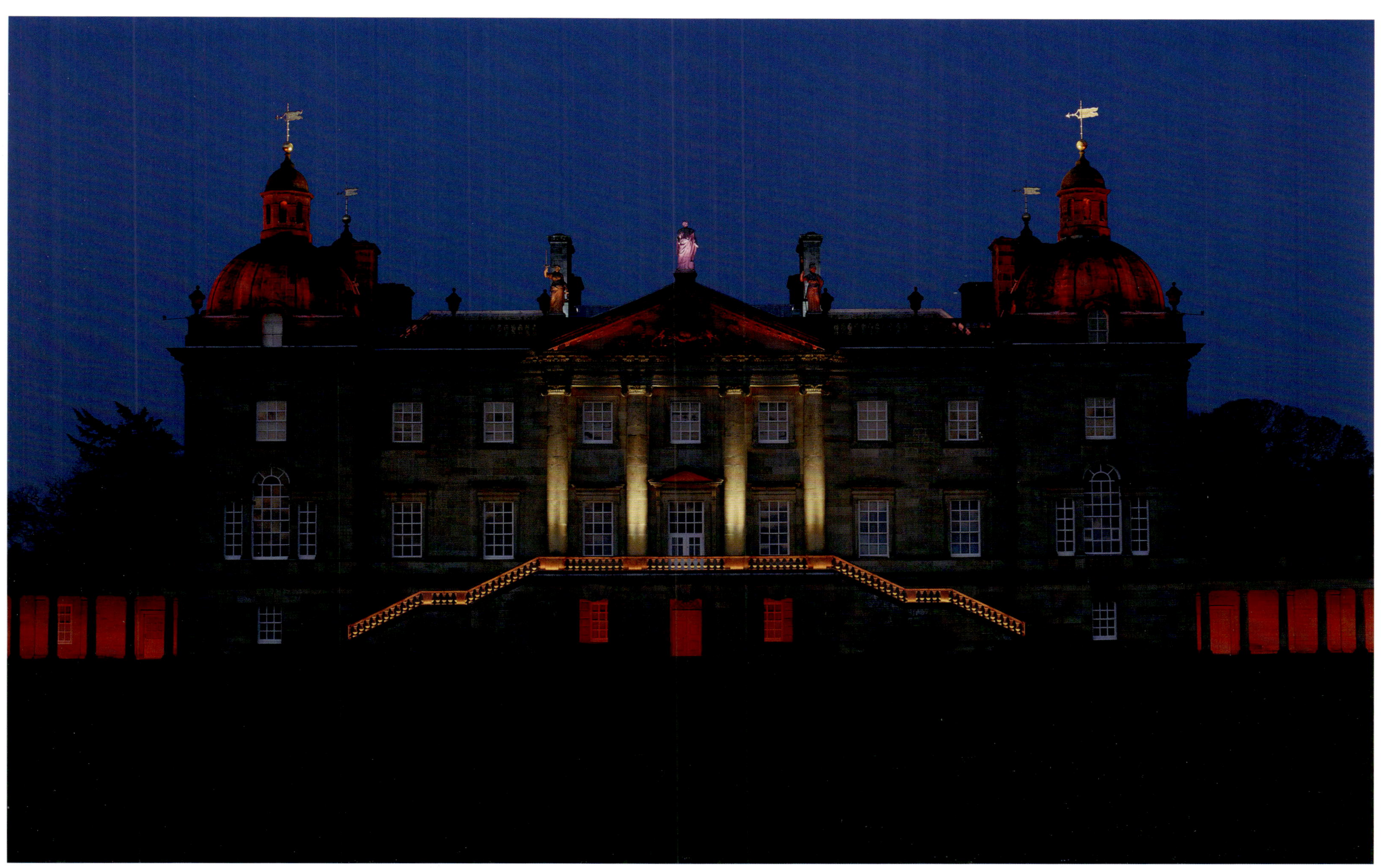

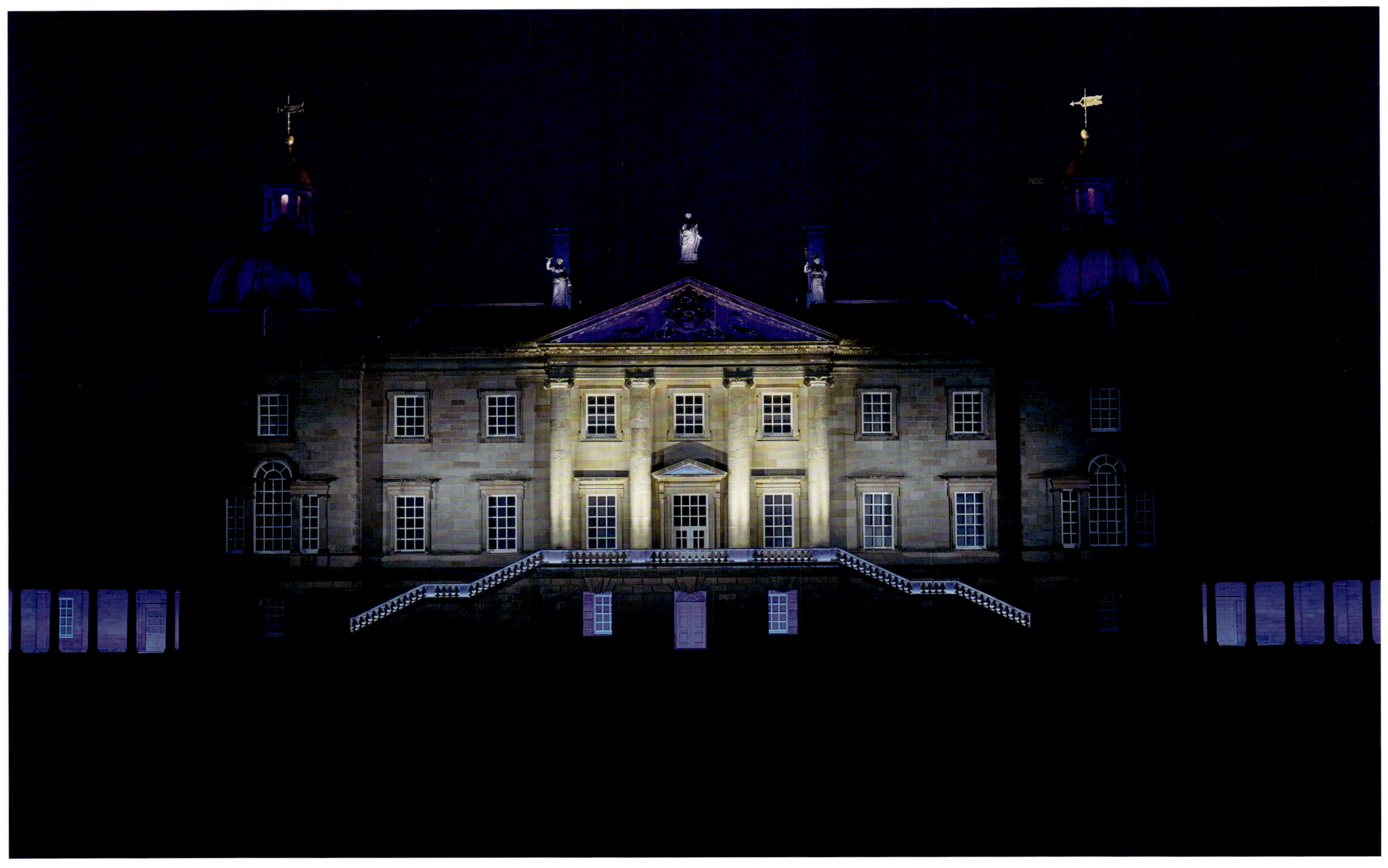

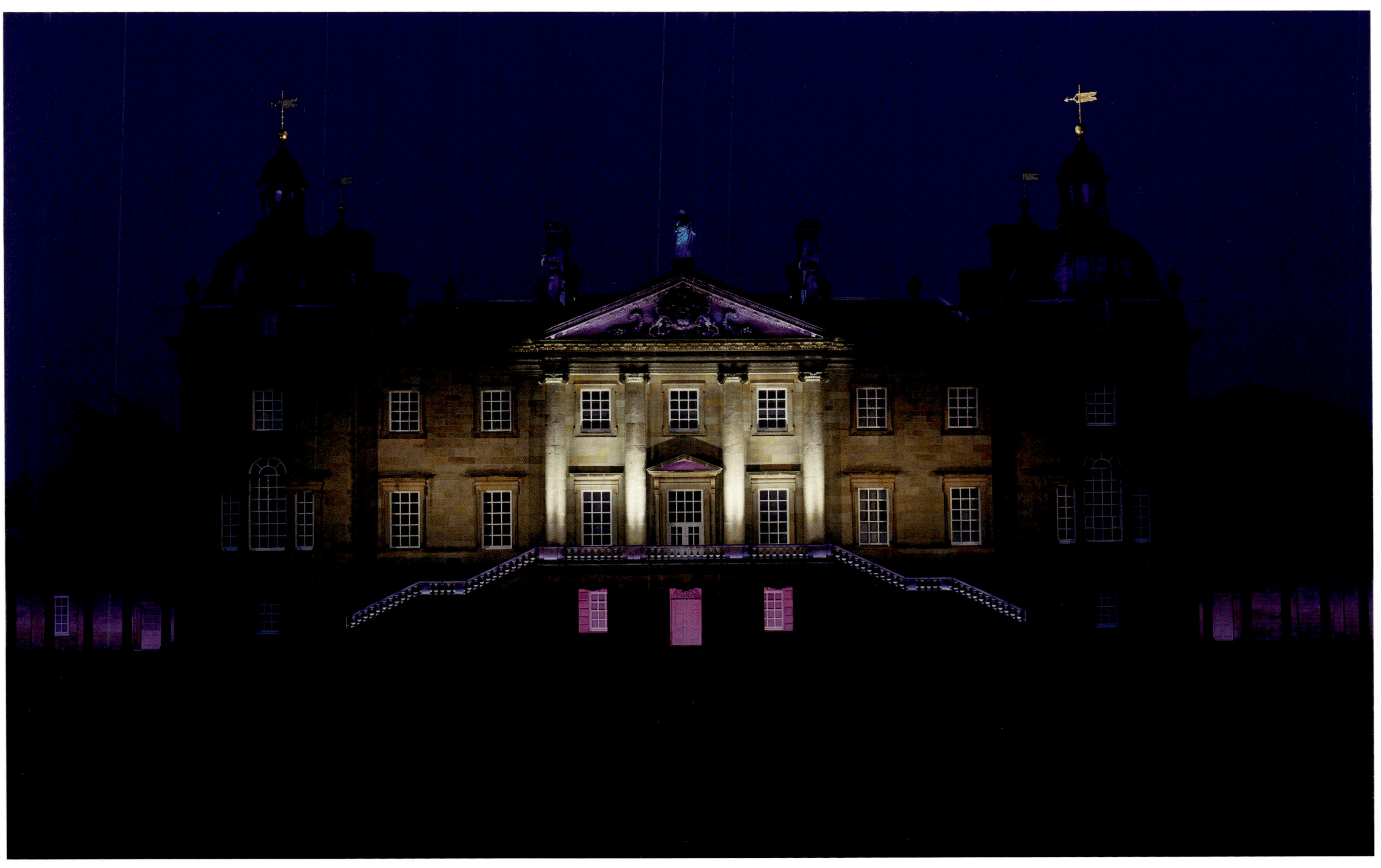

Seldom Seen, 2002

Skyspace exterior

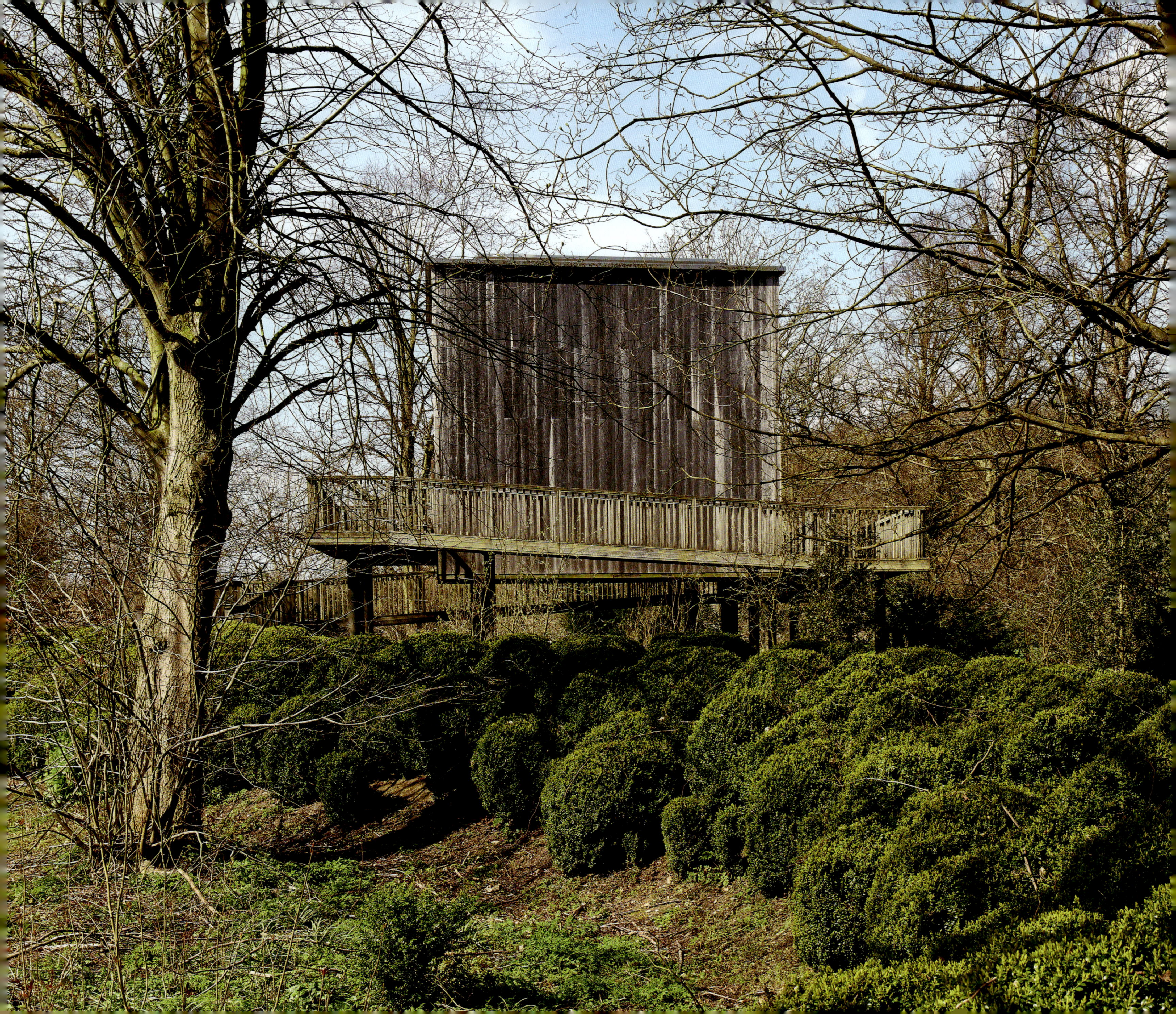

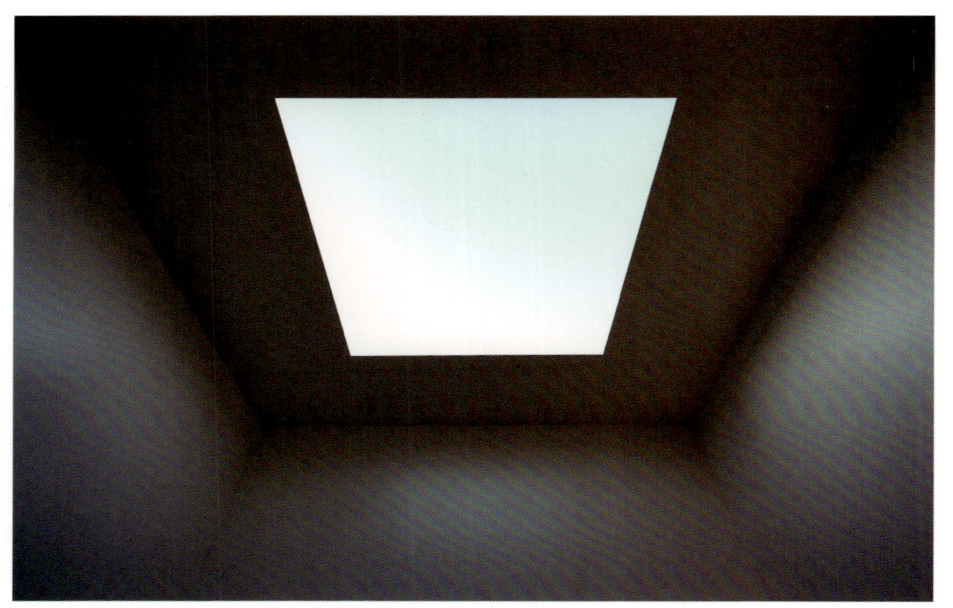

Seldom Seen, 2002

Skyspace interior

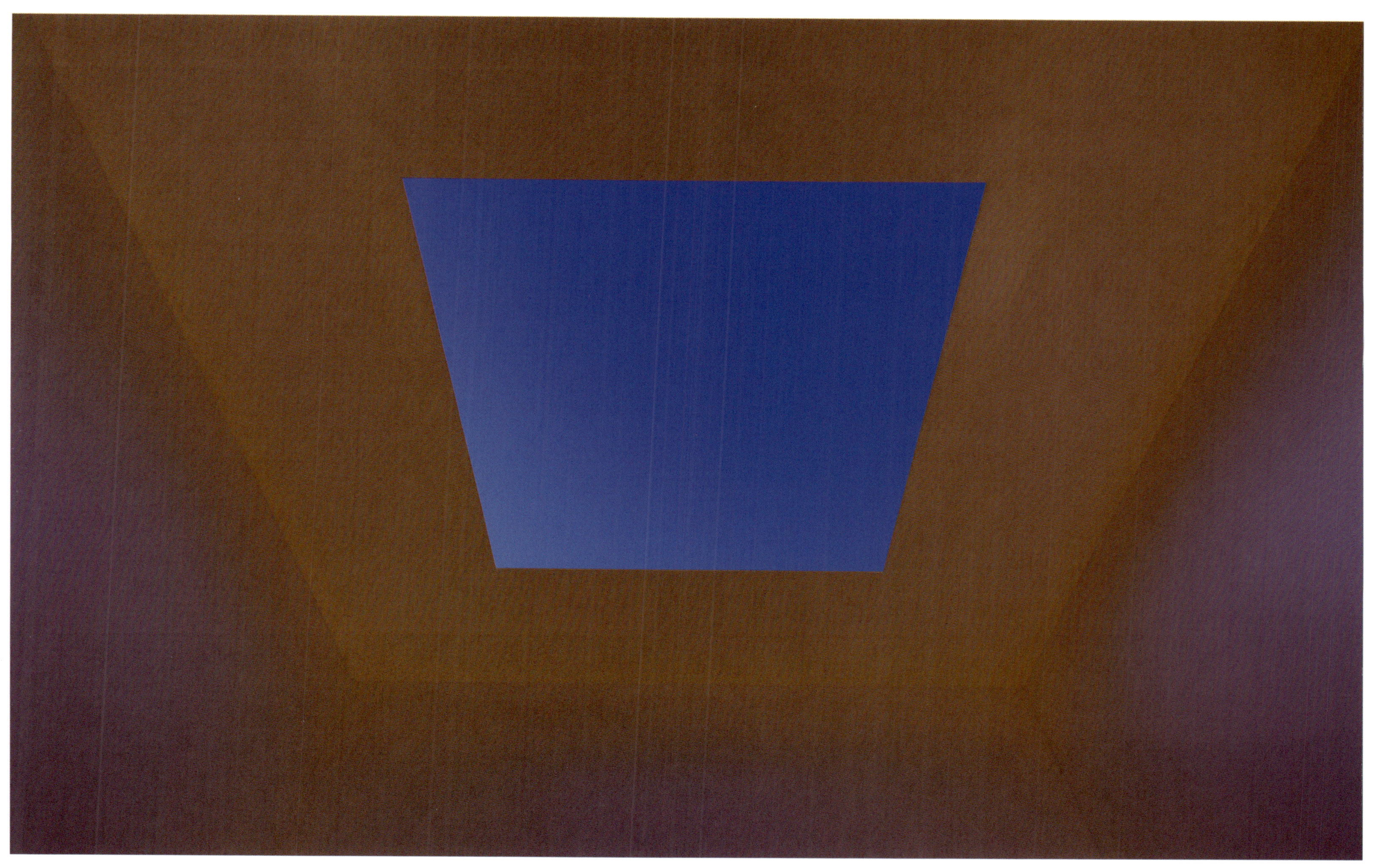

Seldom Seen, 2002

Skyspace interior

Water tower, Houghton Park

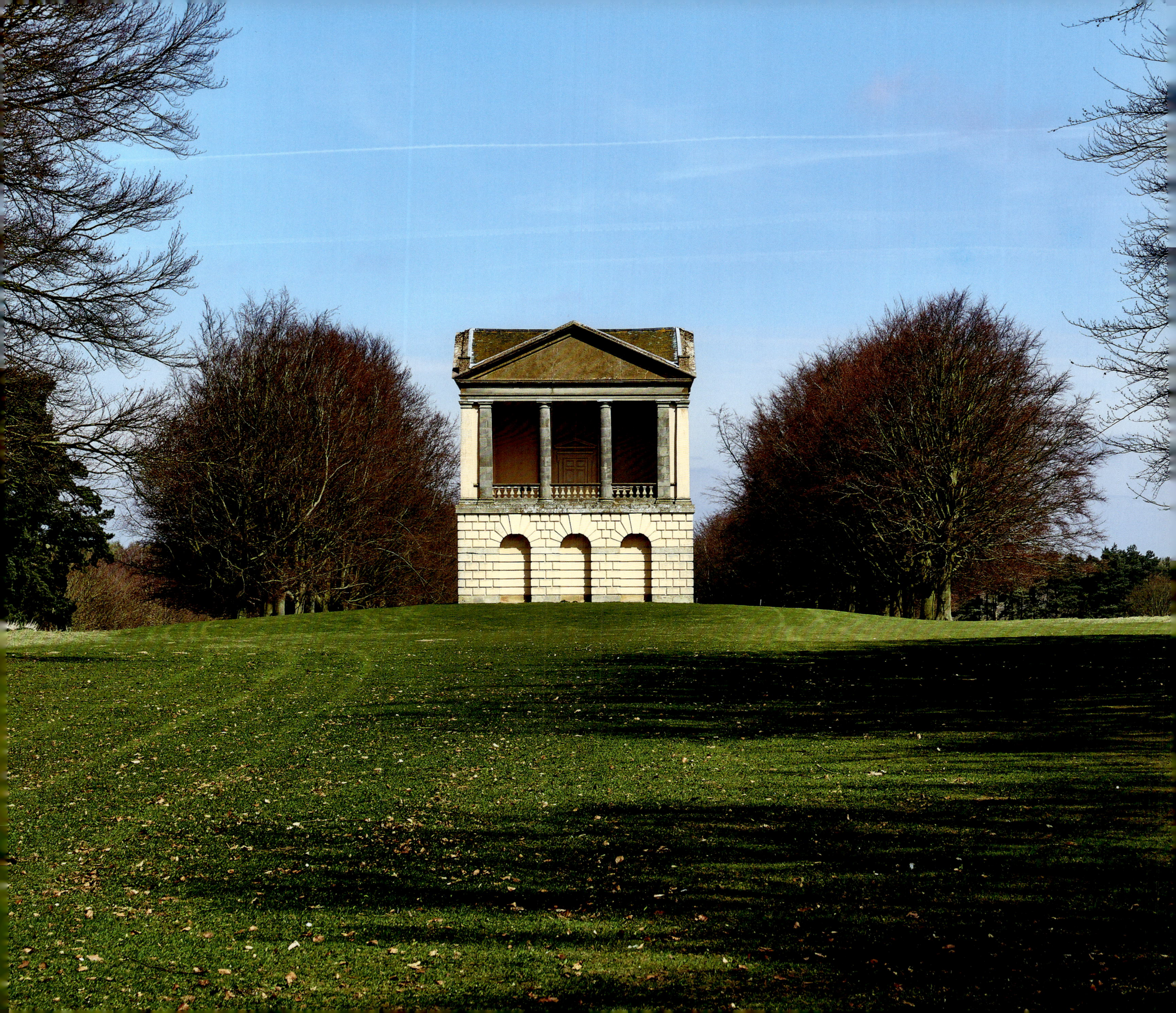

St Elmo's Breath, 1992

Interior of water tower, Houghton Park

Raemar Magenta, 1970

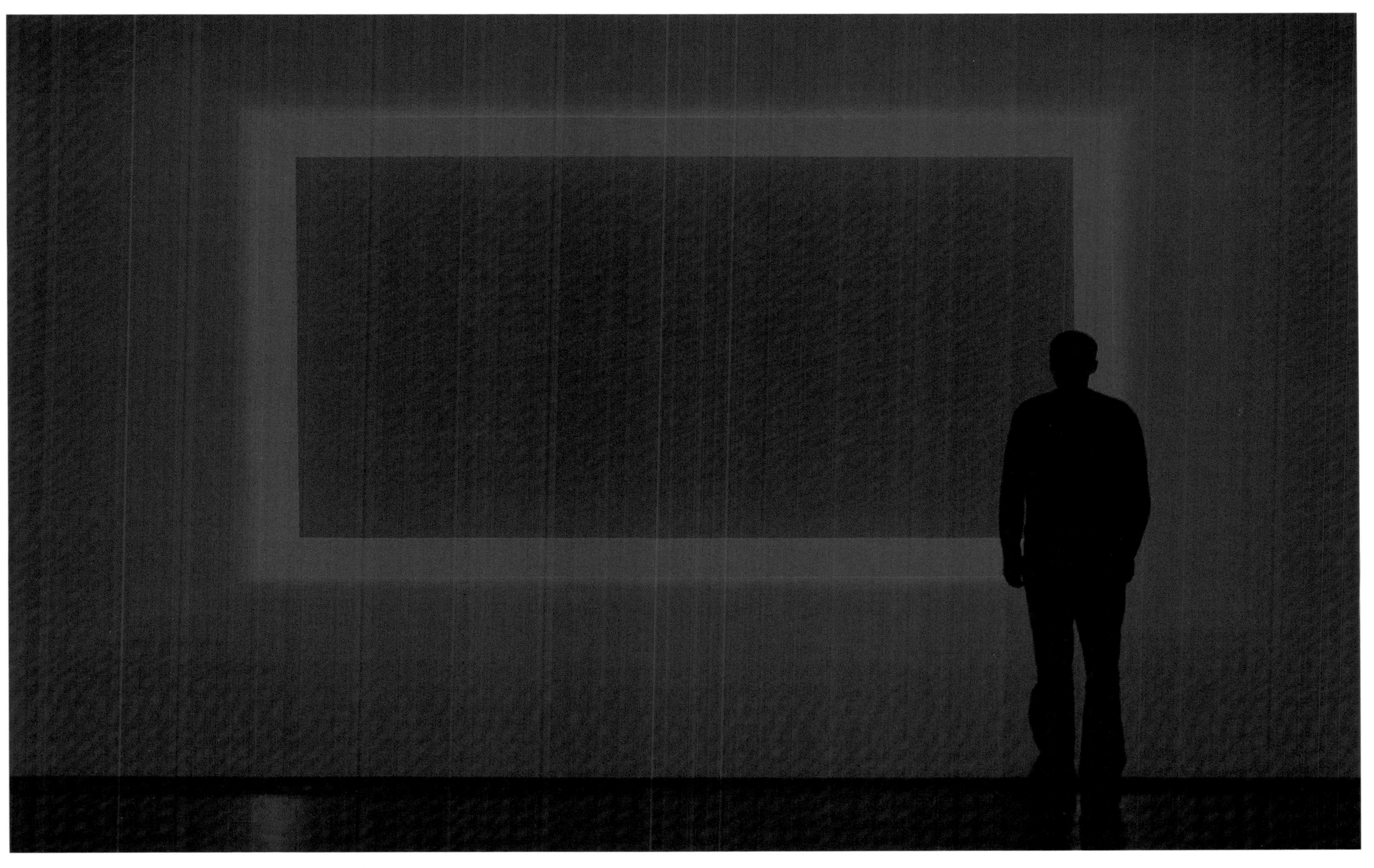

Raethro, Red, 1968

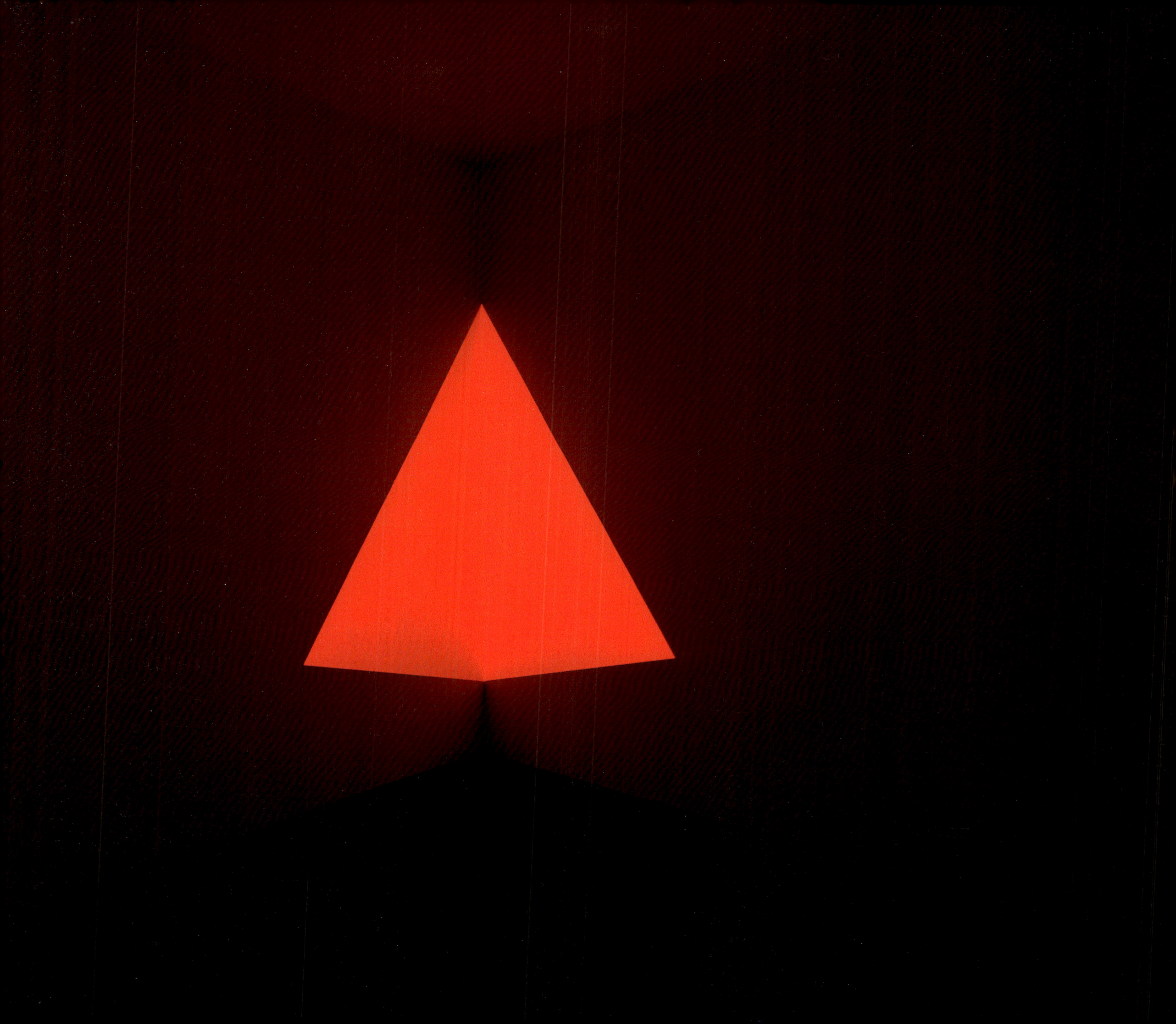

Enzu, Green, 1968

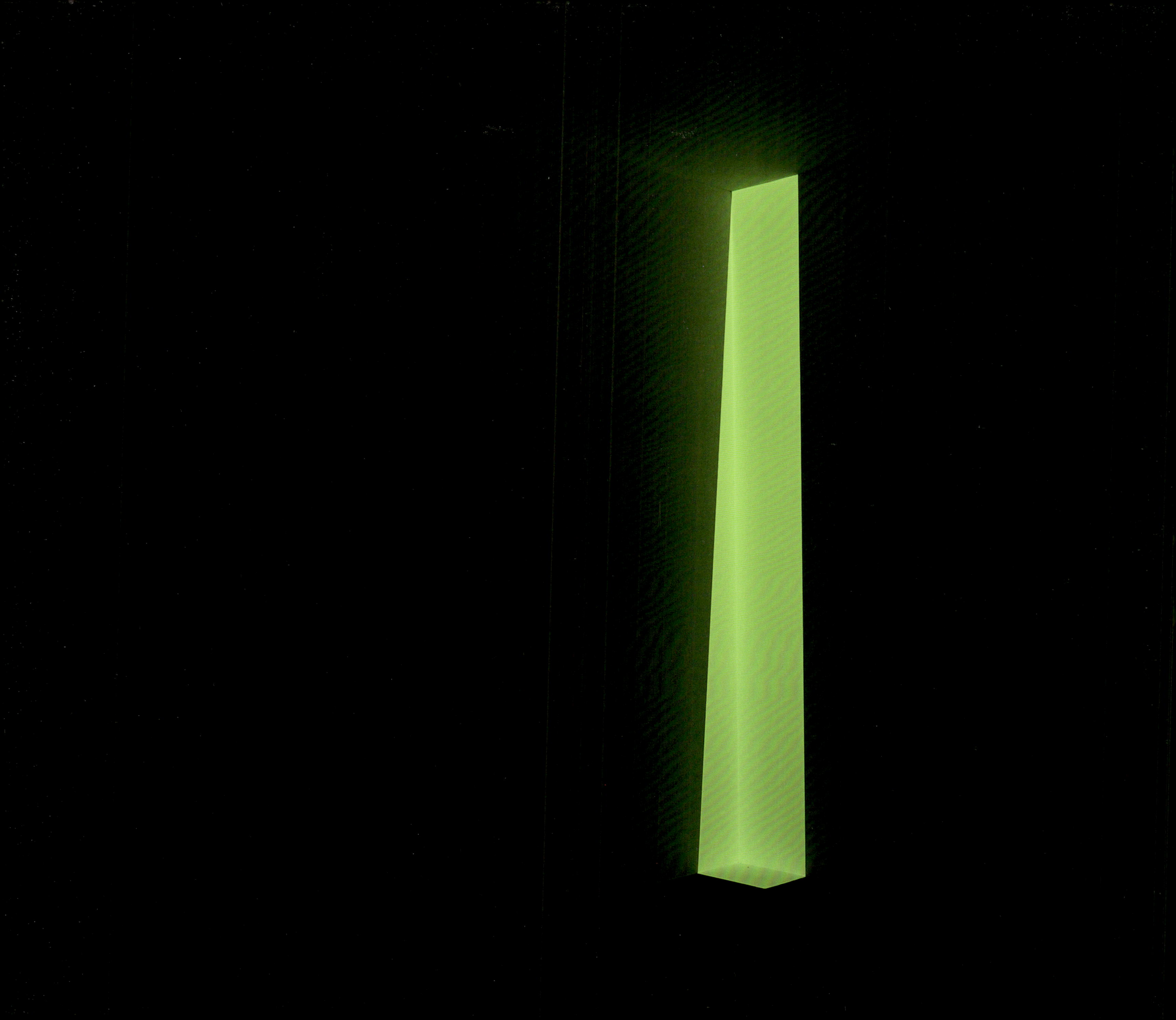

Shirim, 2015

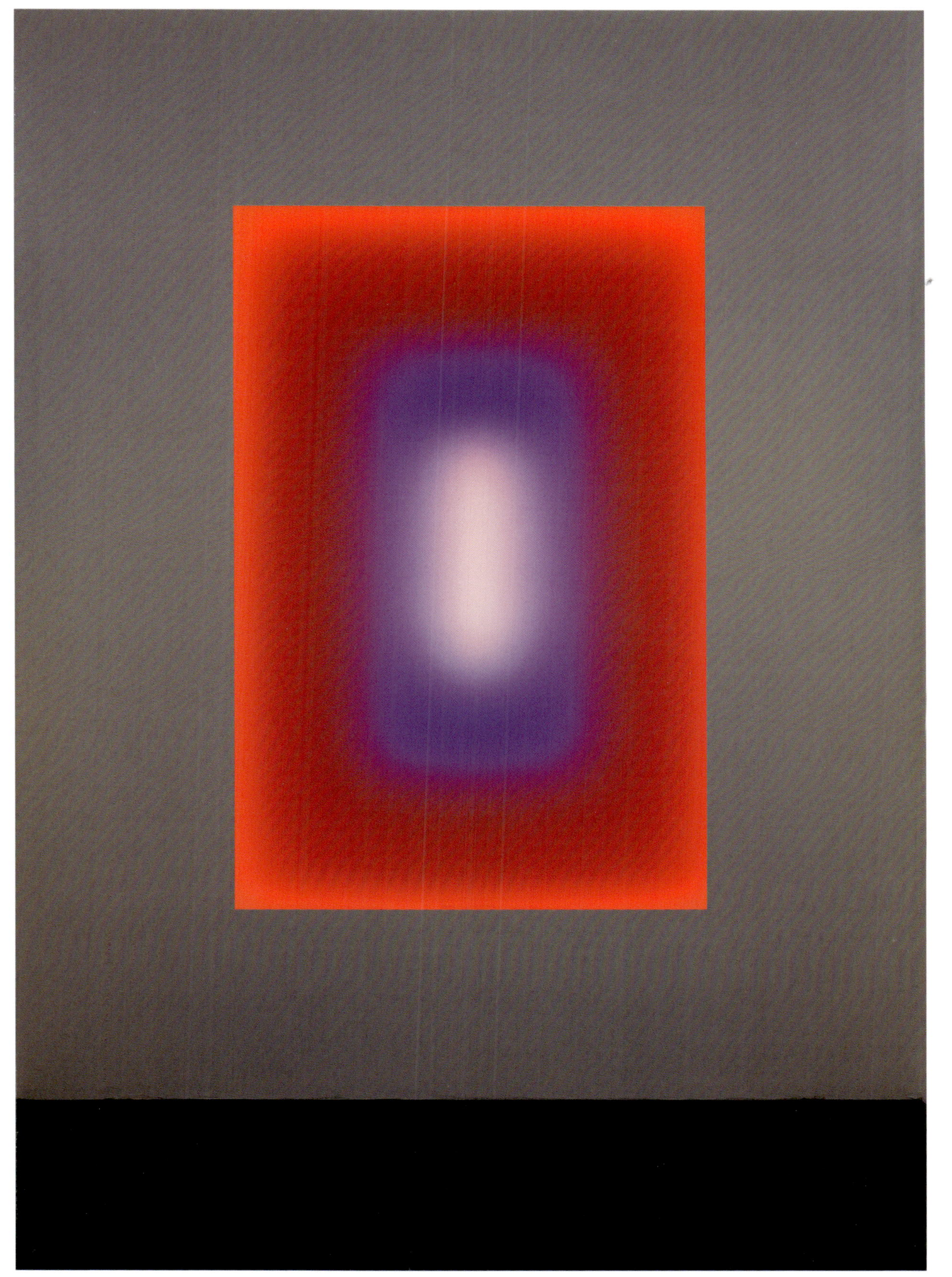

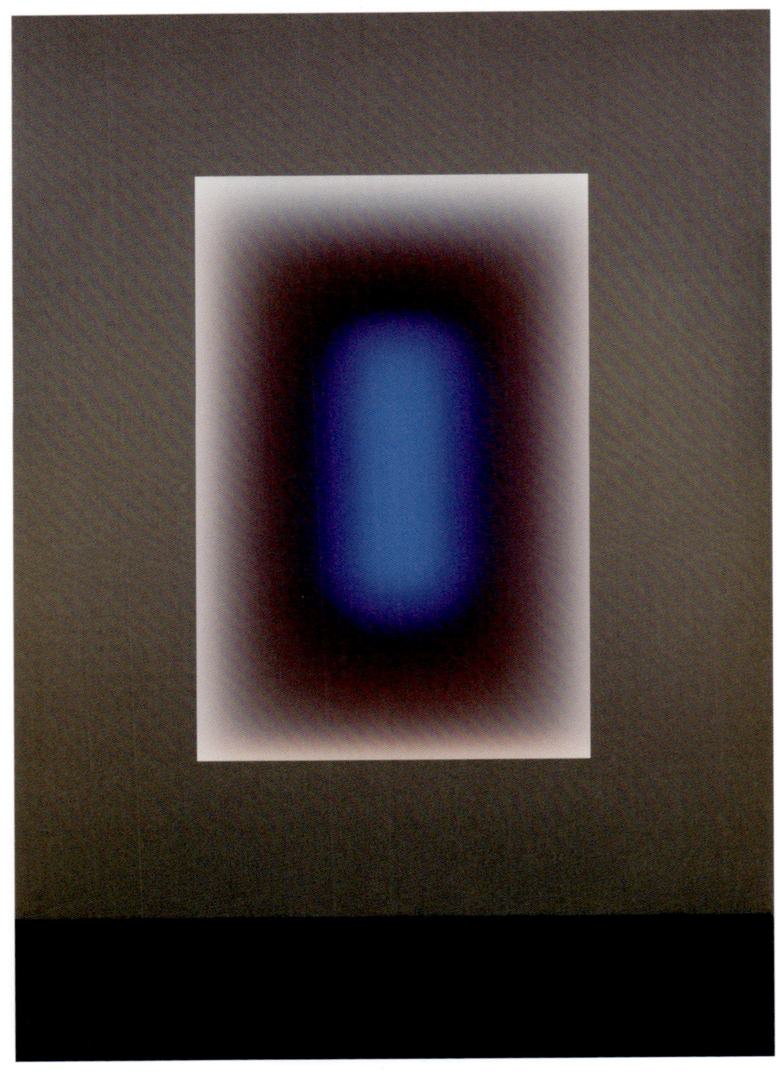

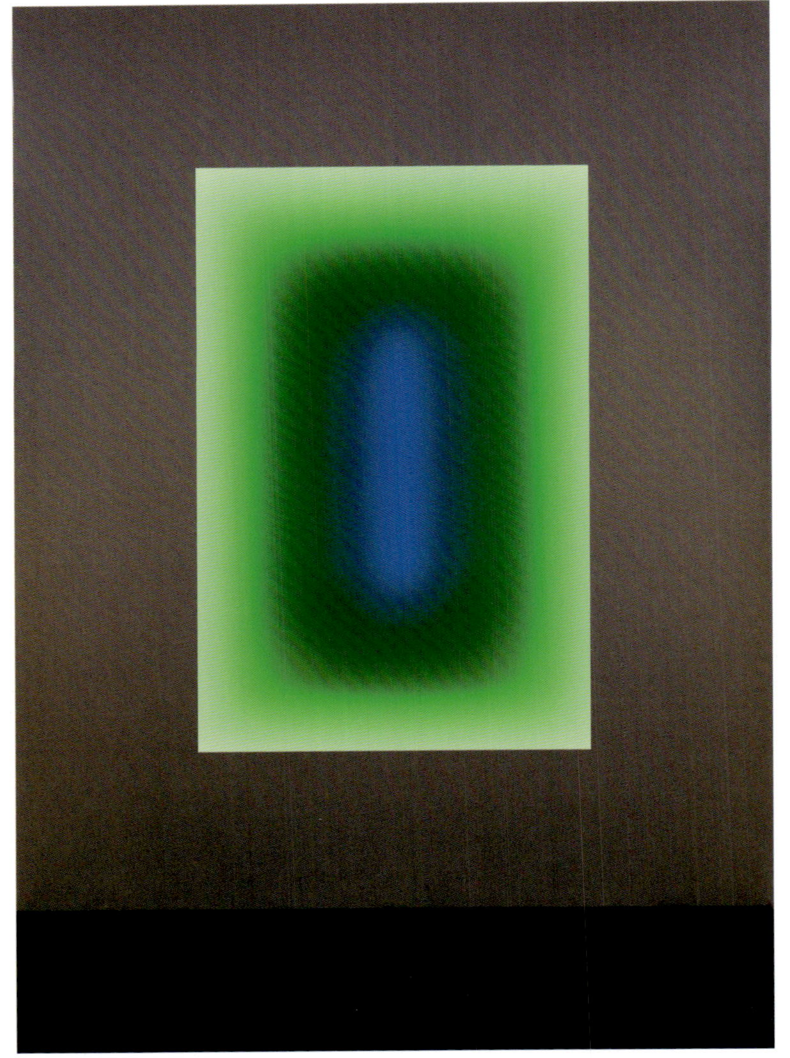

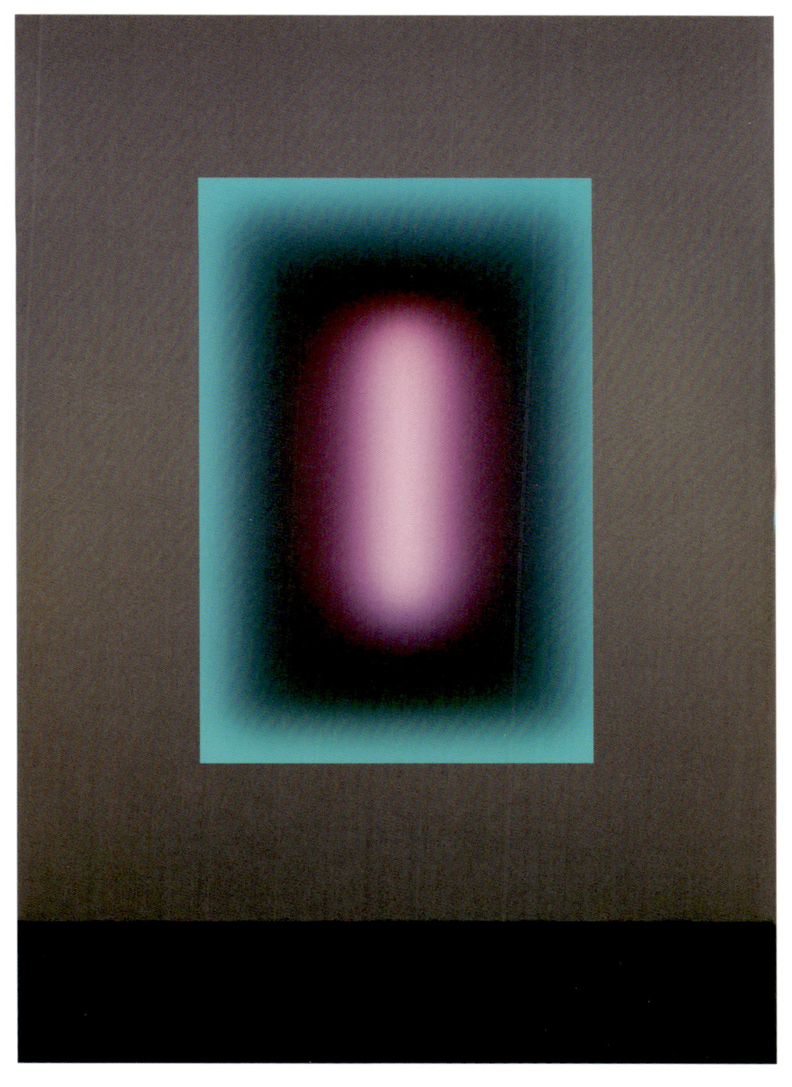

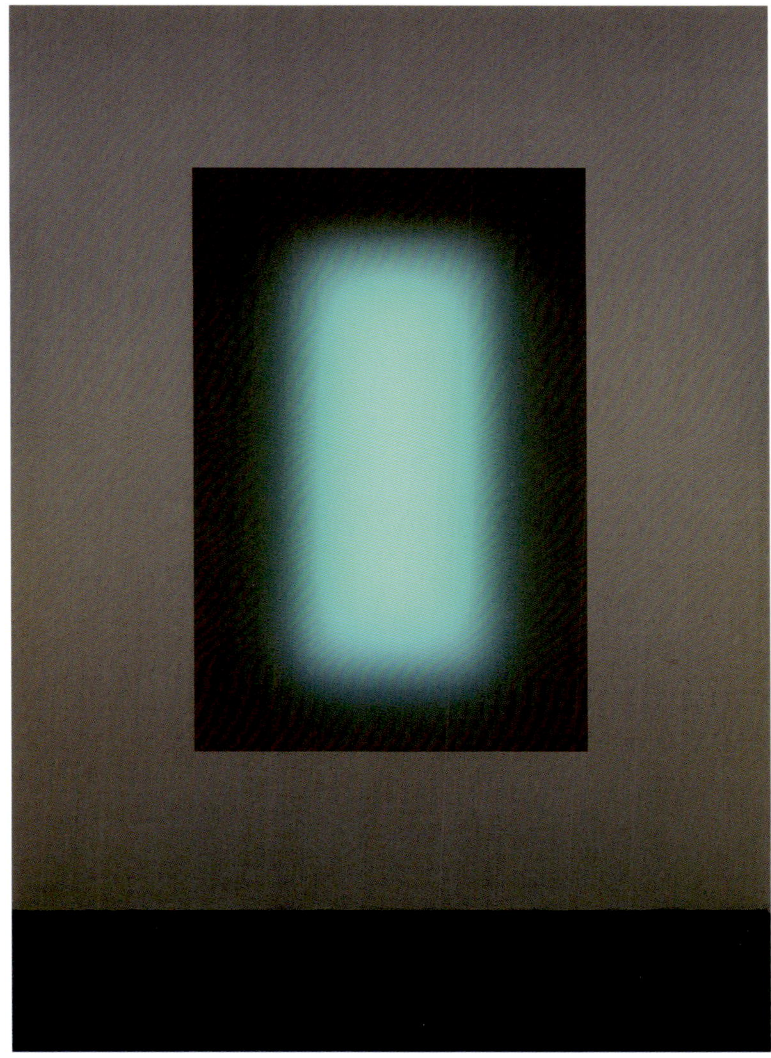

Tortoise Beats Hare, 2015

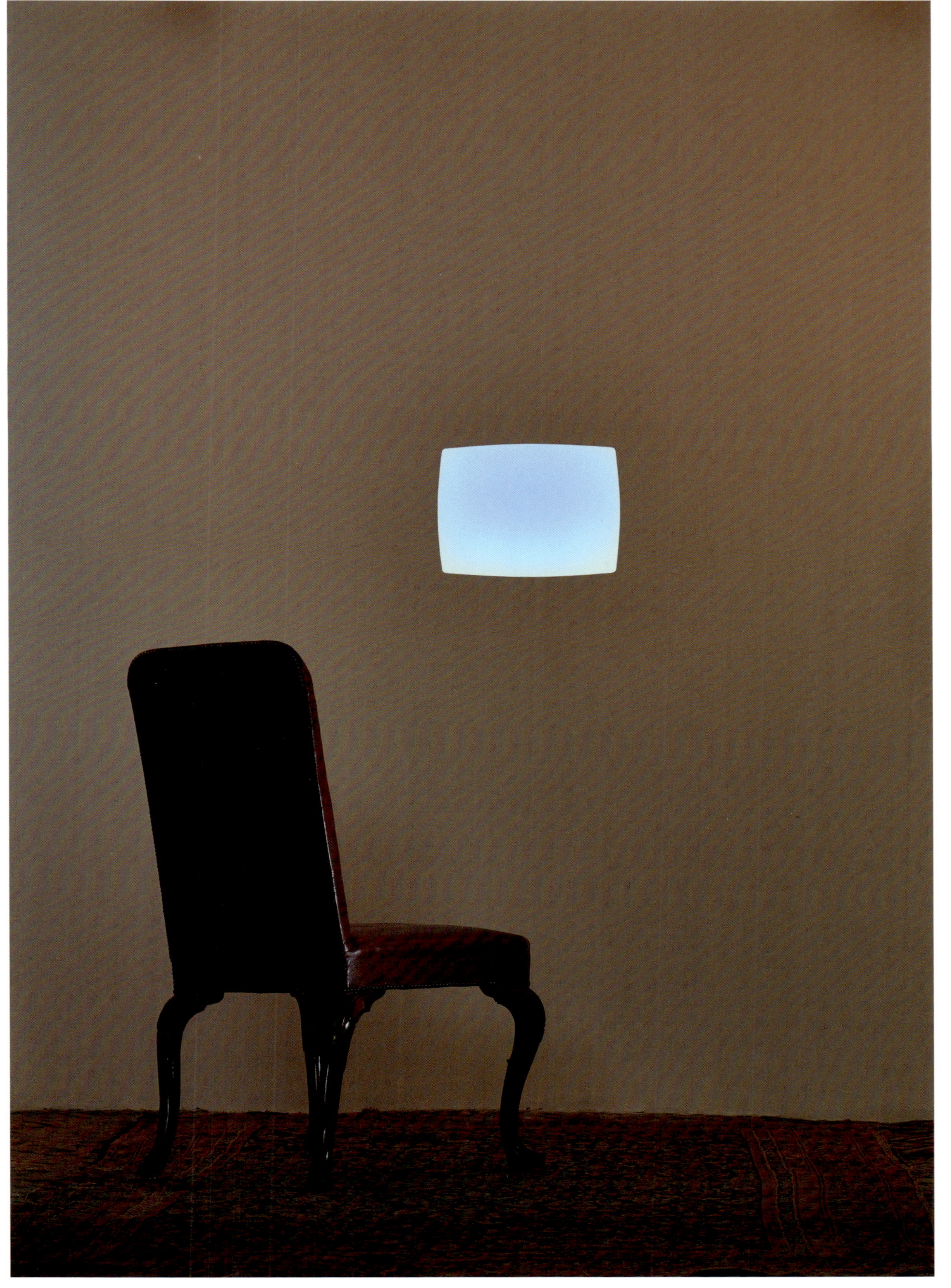

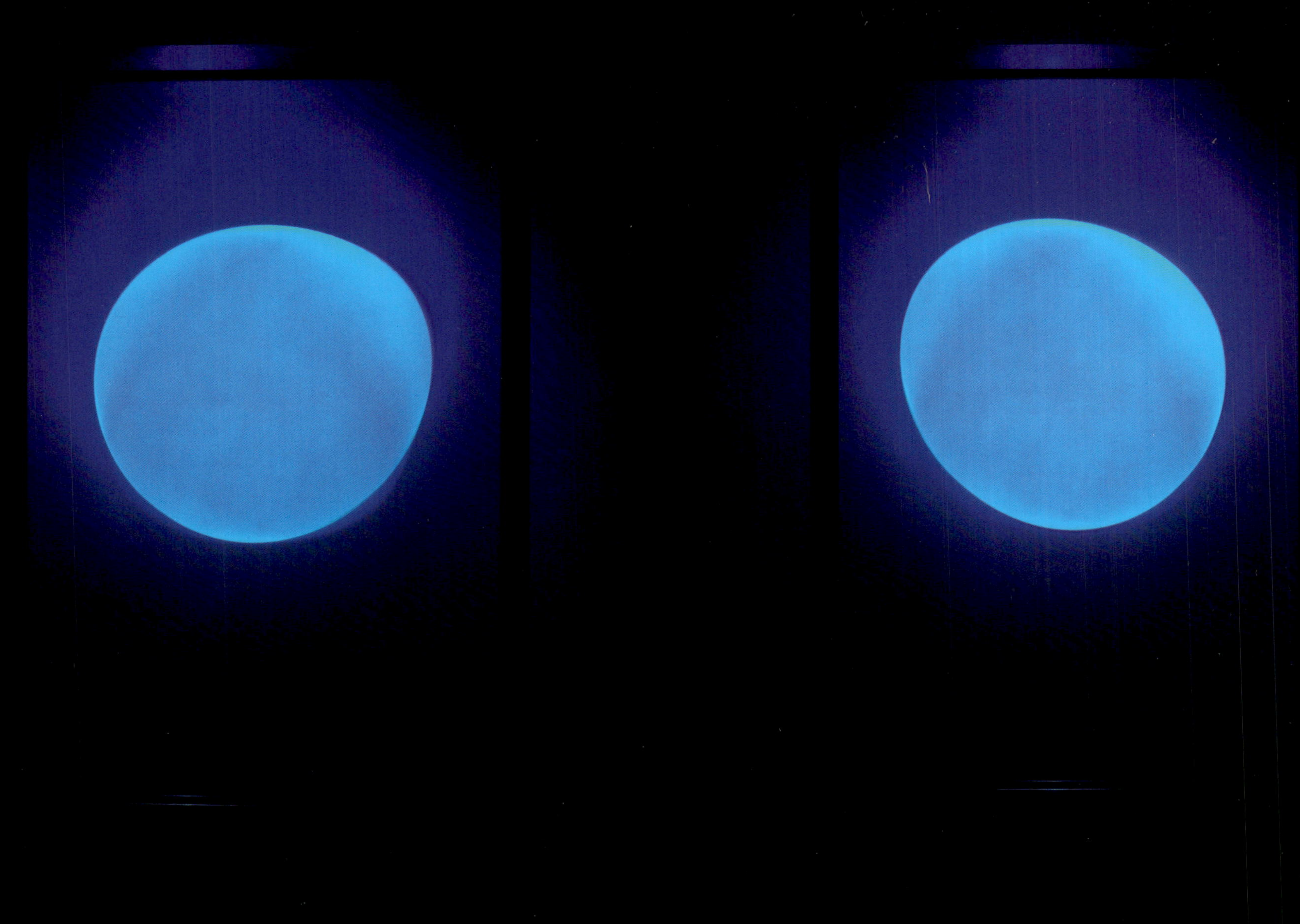

Untitled, 2010

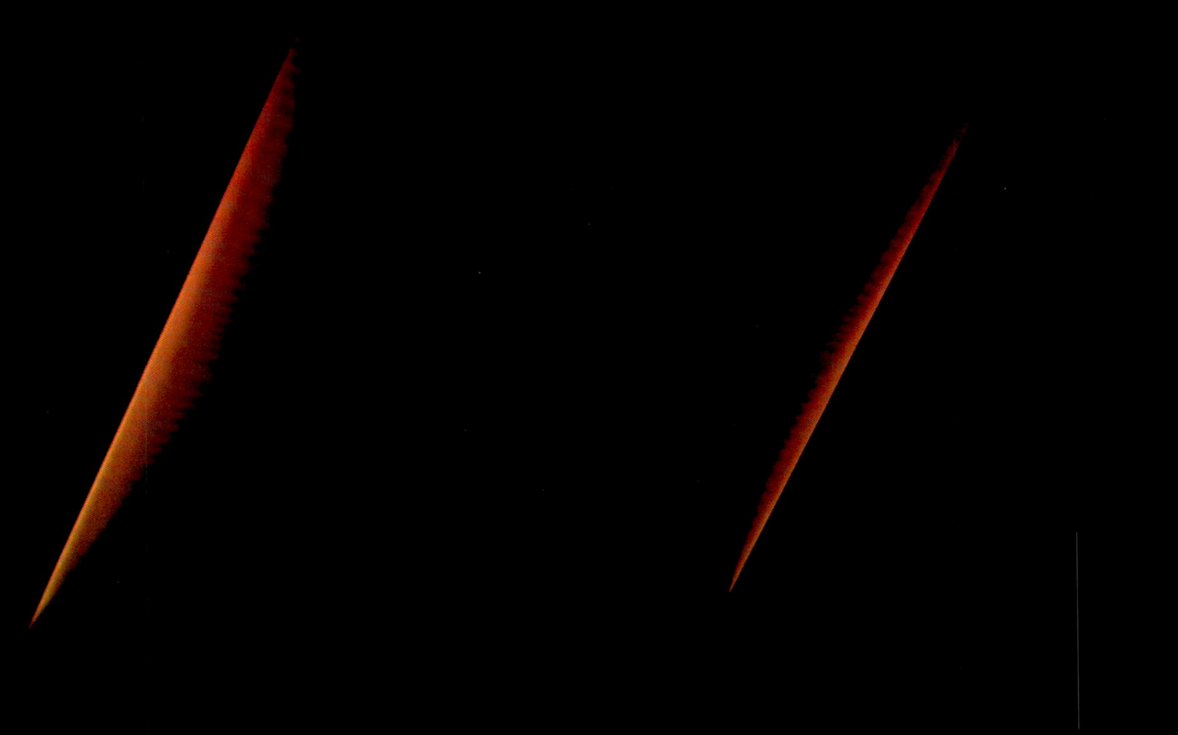

Untitled, No. XXVG, 2008

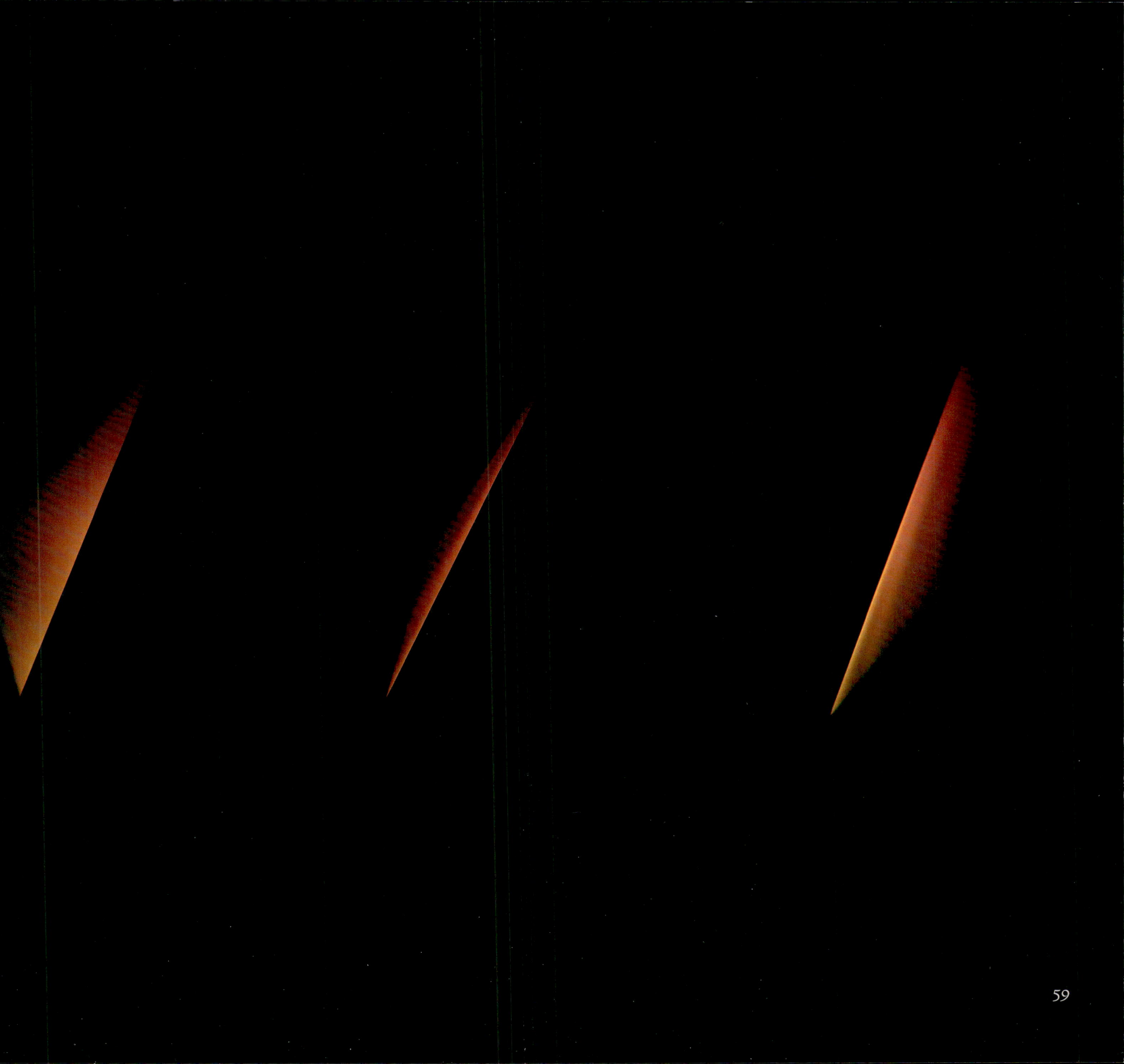

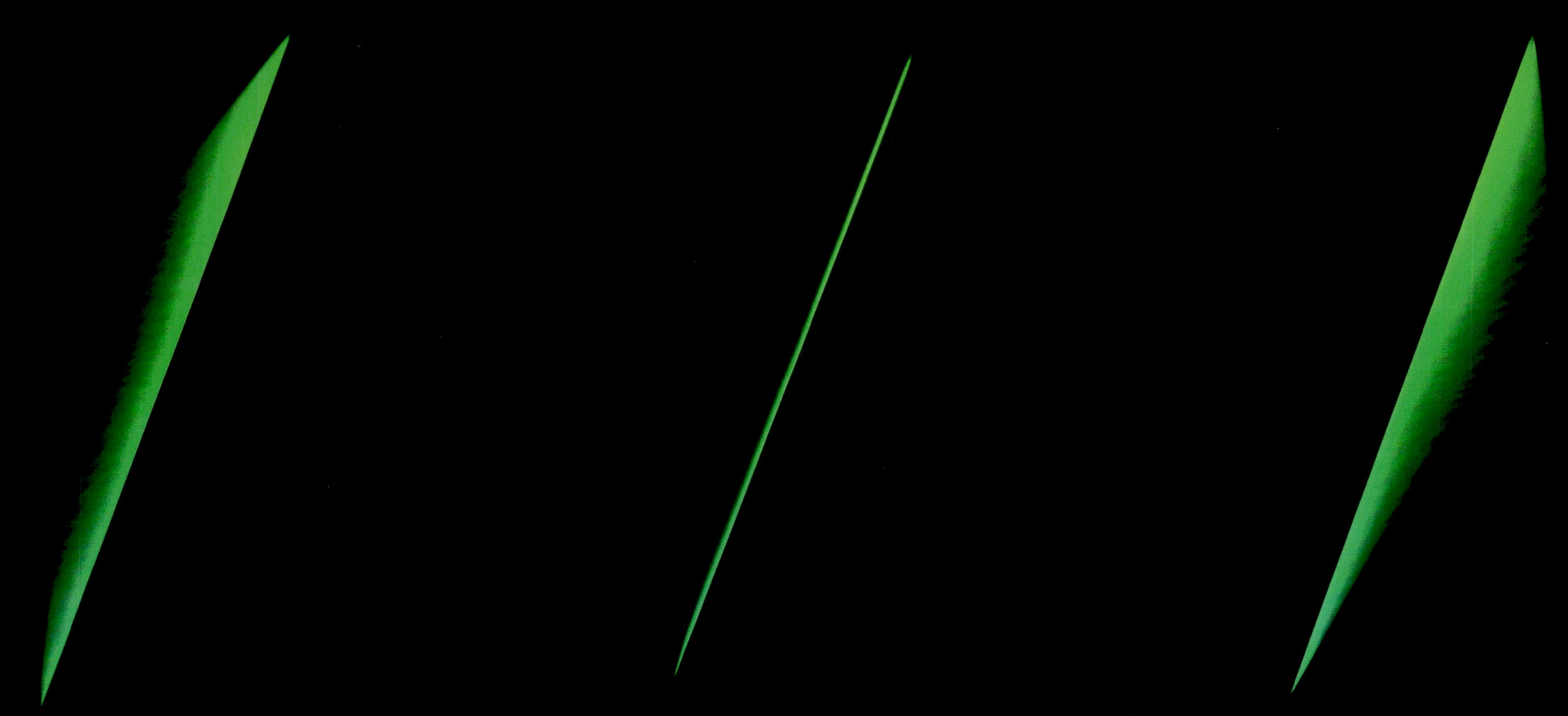

Untitled, No. XXX, 2012

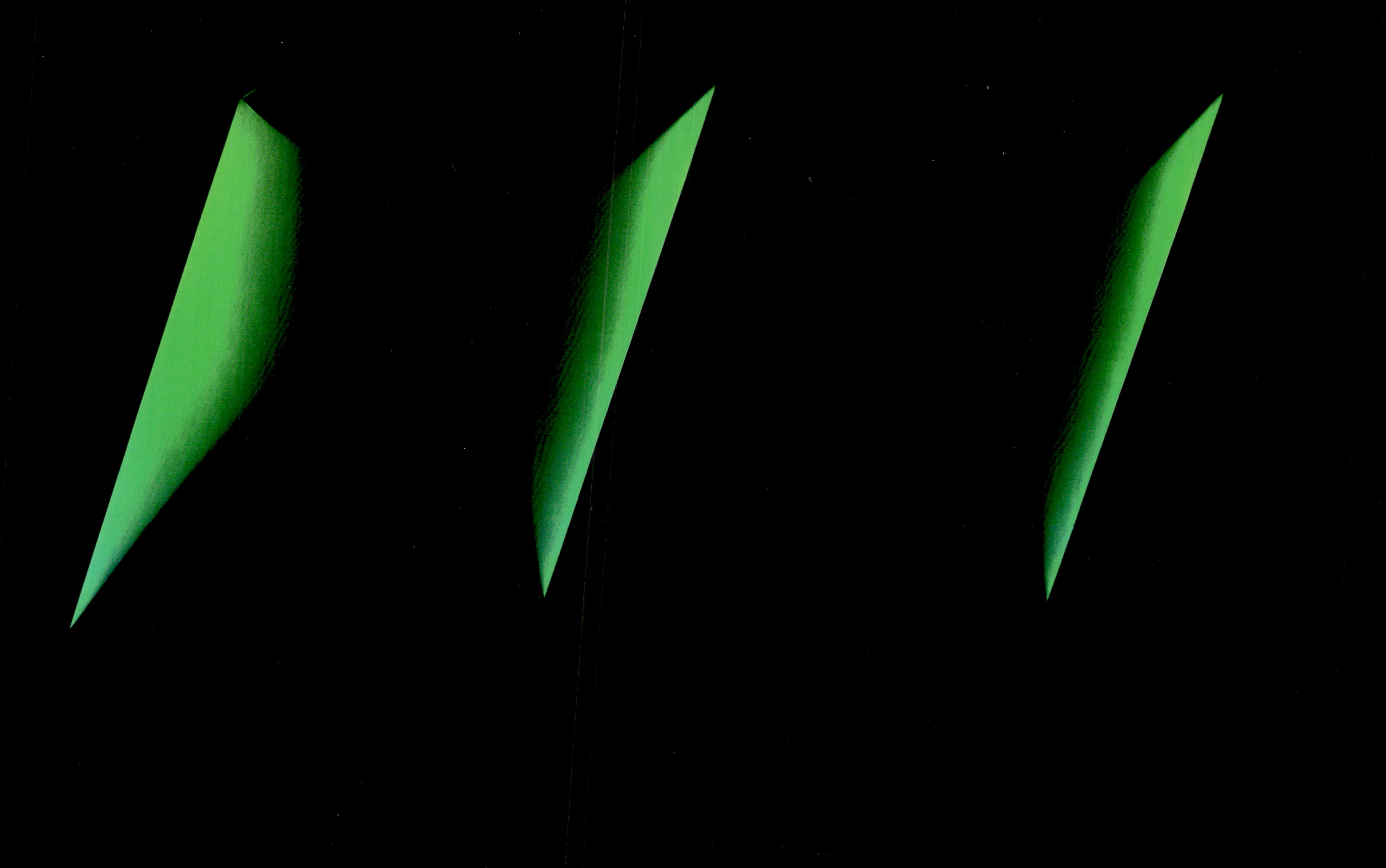

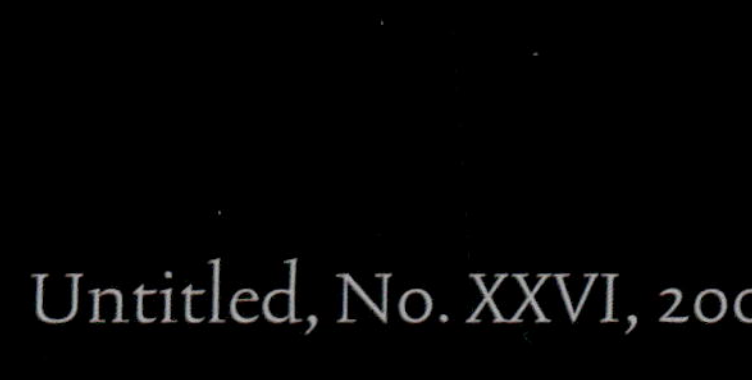

Untitled, No. XXVI, 200

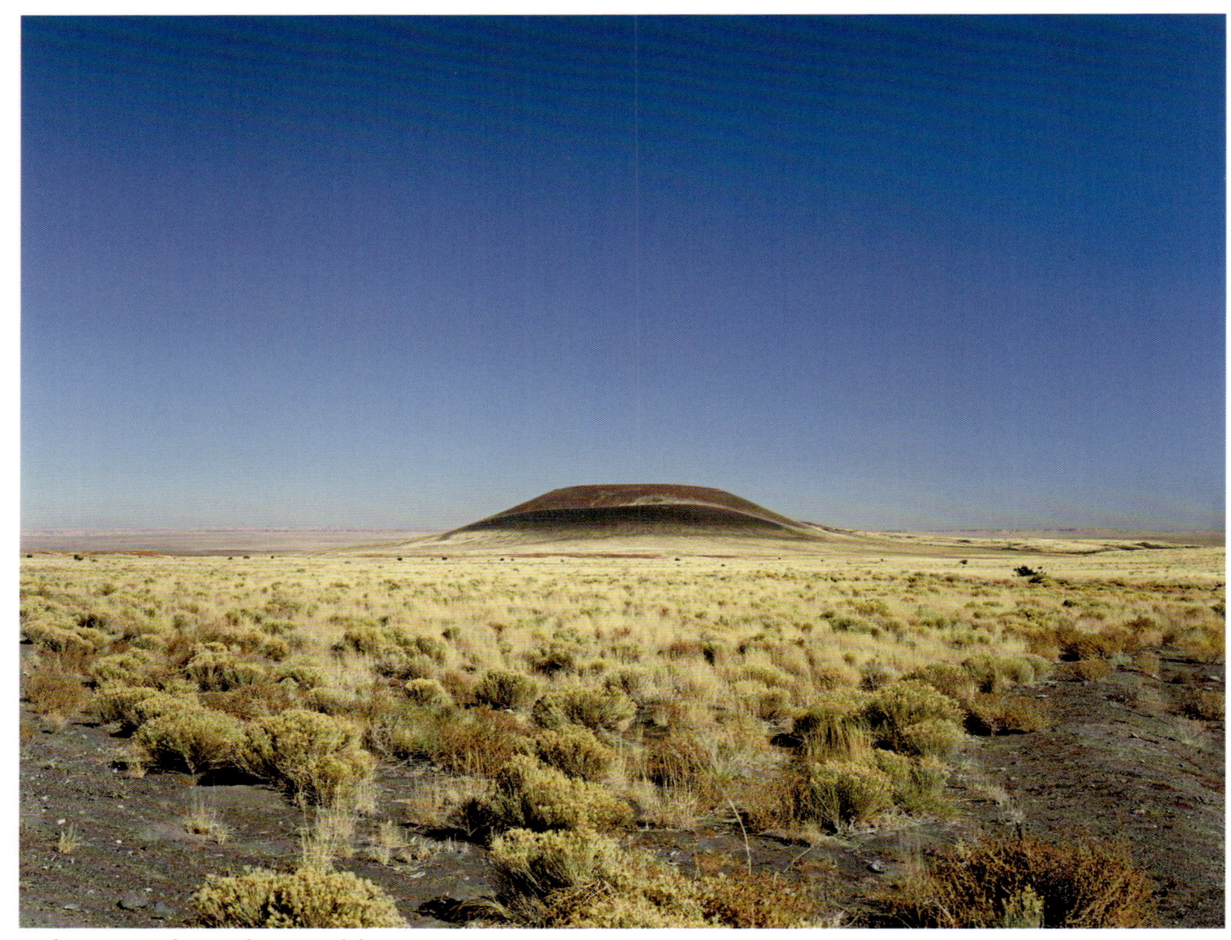

Roden Crater. Photo: Florian Holzherr

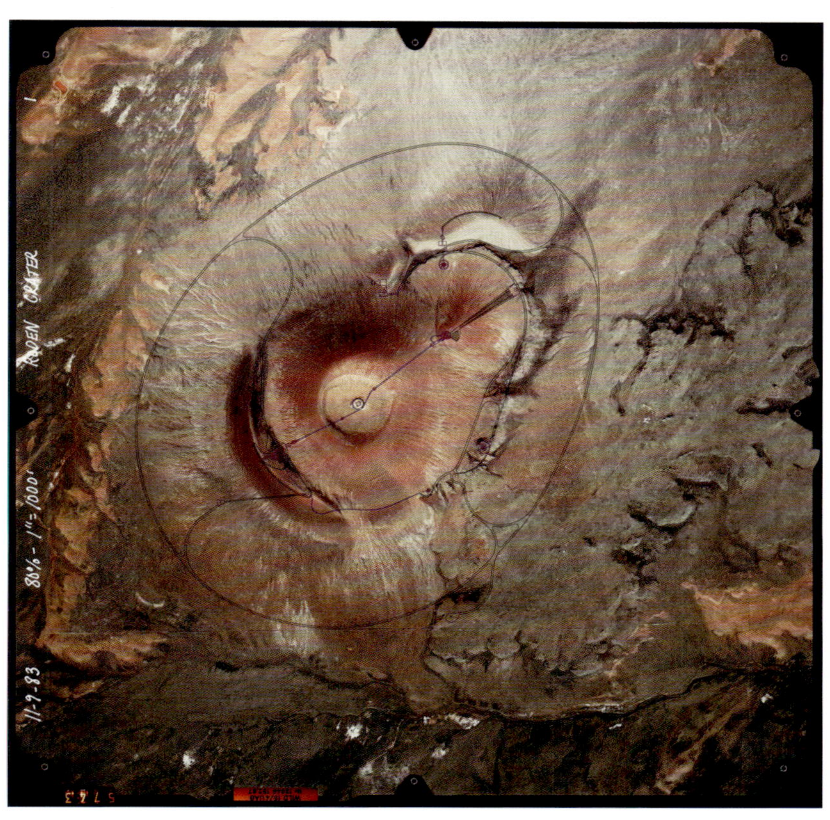

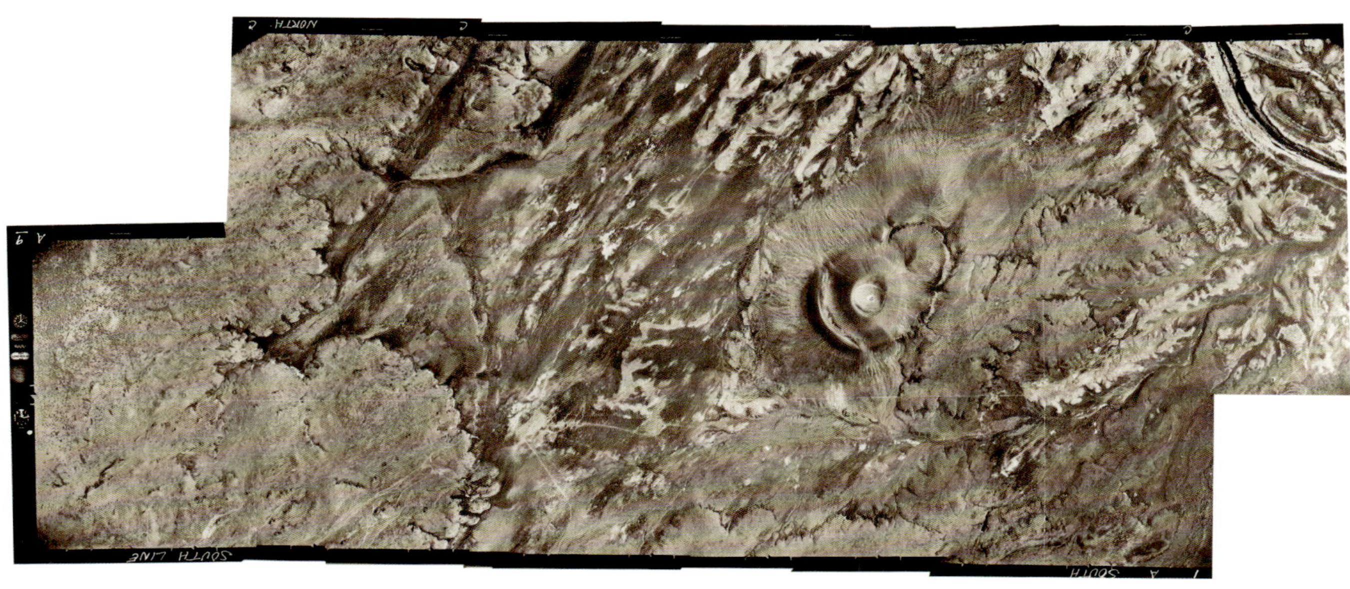

My First Roden Crater Photo, 2010

Roden Crater, 2010

East Portal, Roden Crater, 2008

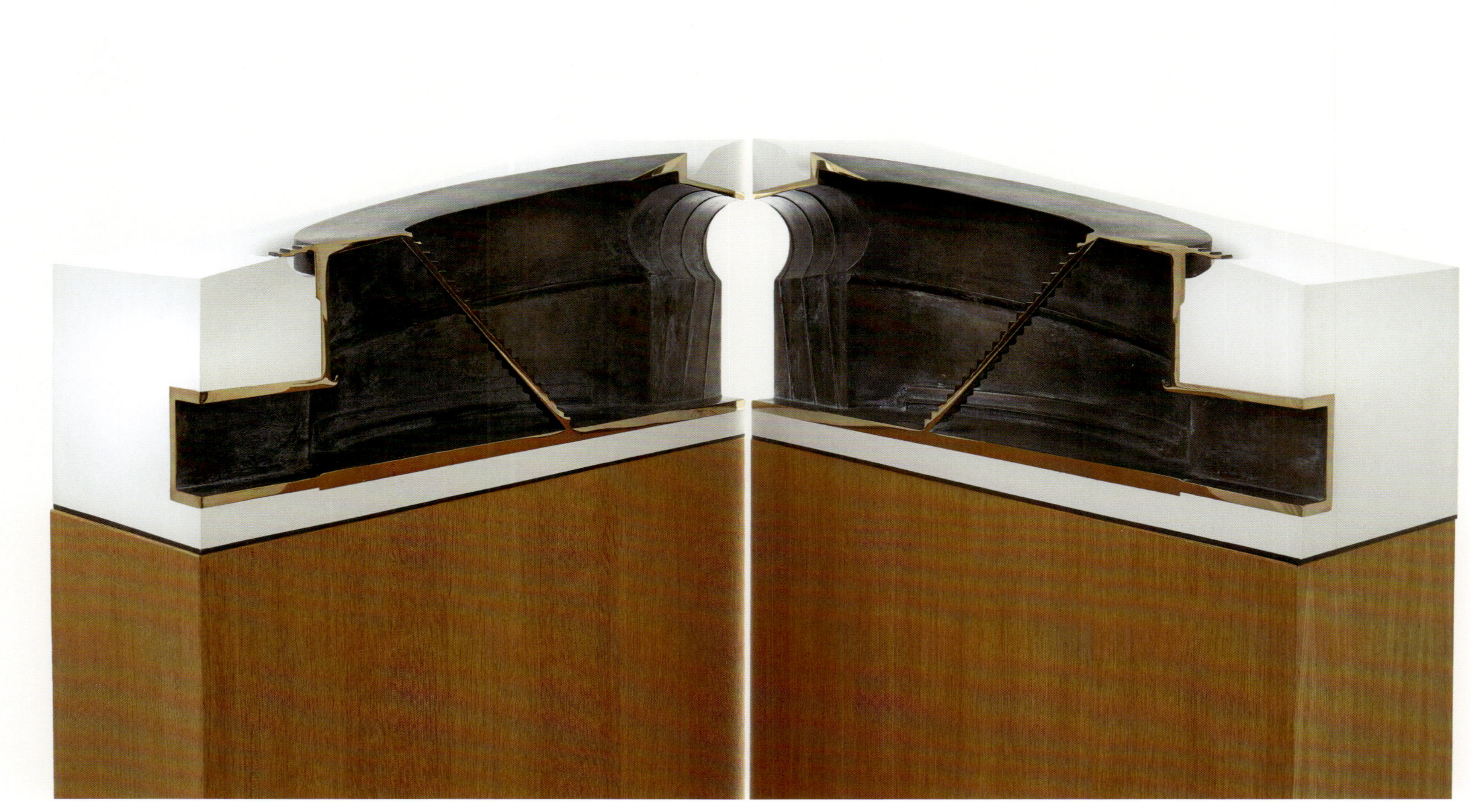

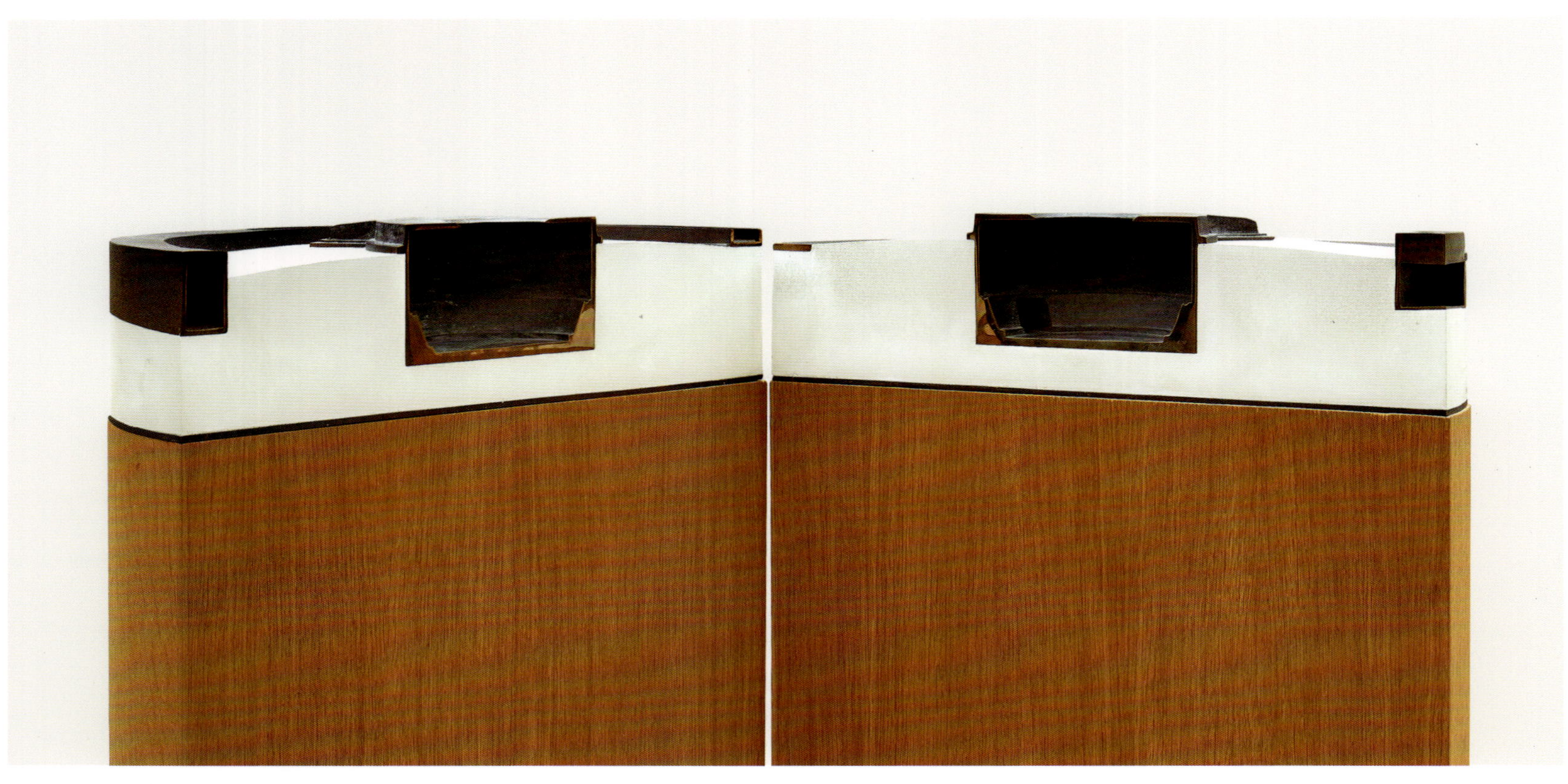

Crater's Eye, Roden Crater, 2008

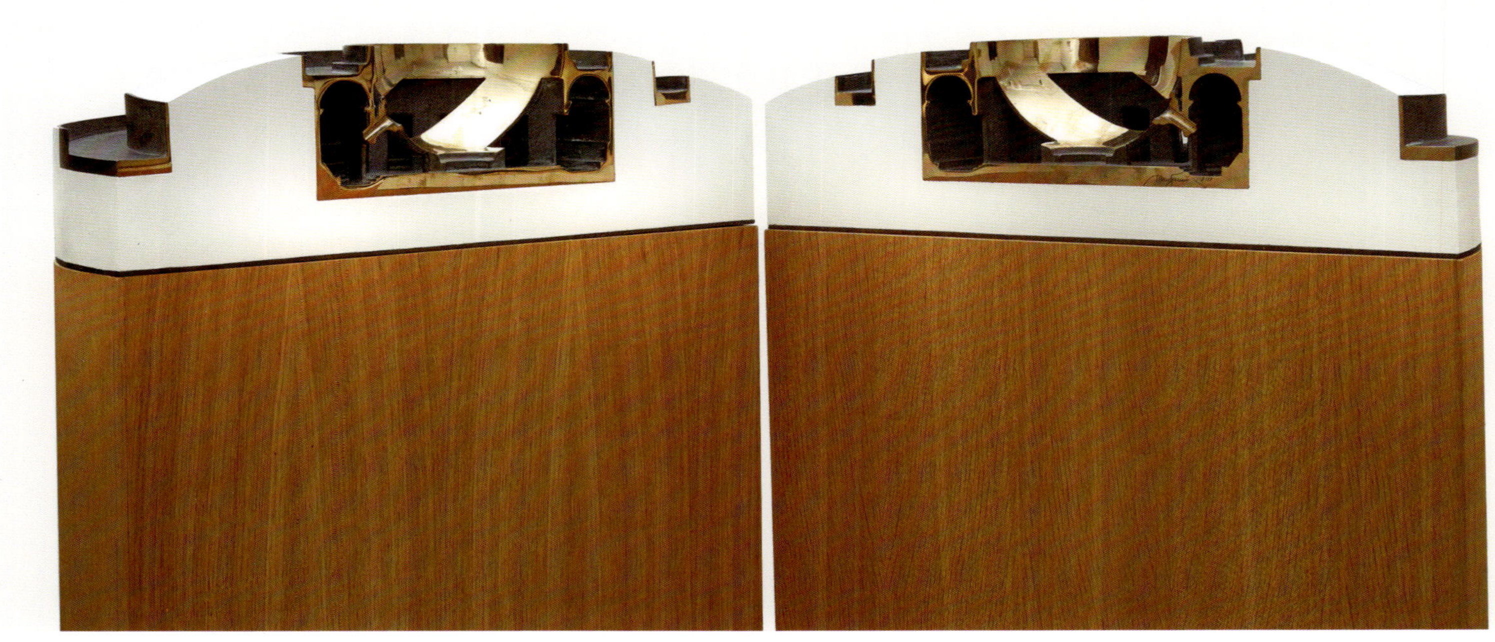

South Space, Roden Crater, 2008

First Light, 1989–90

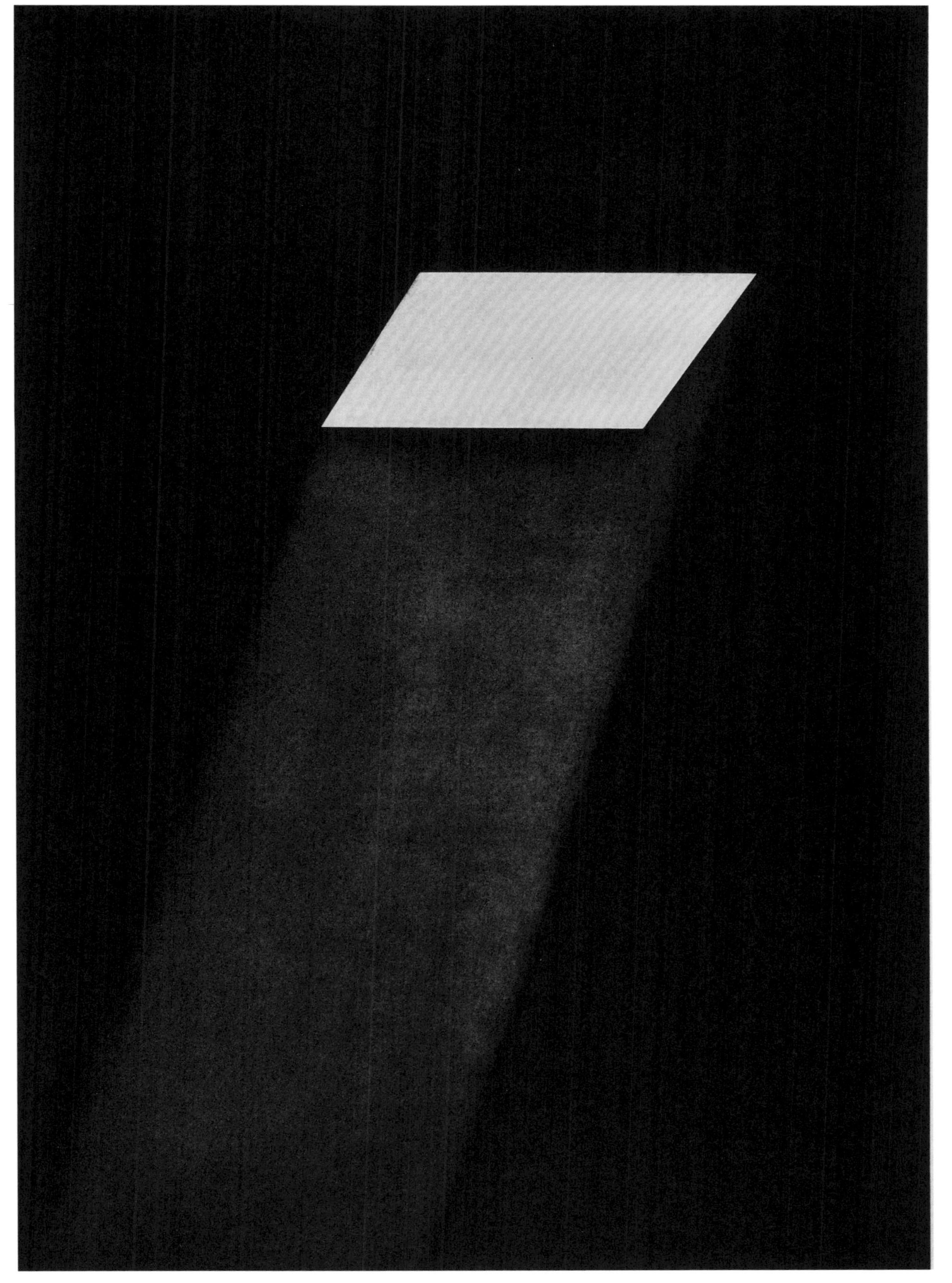

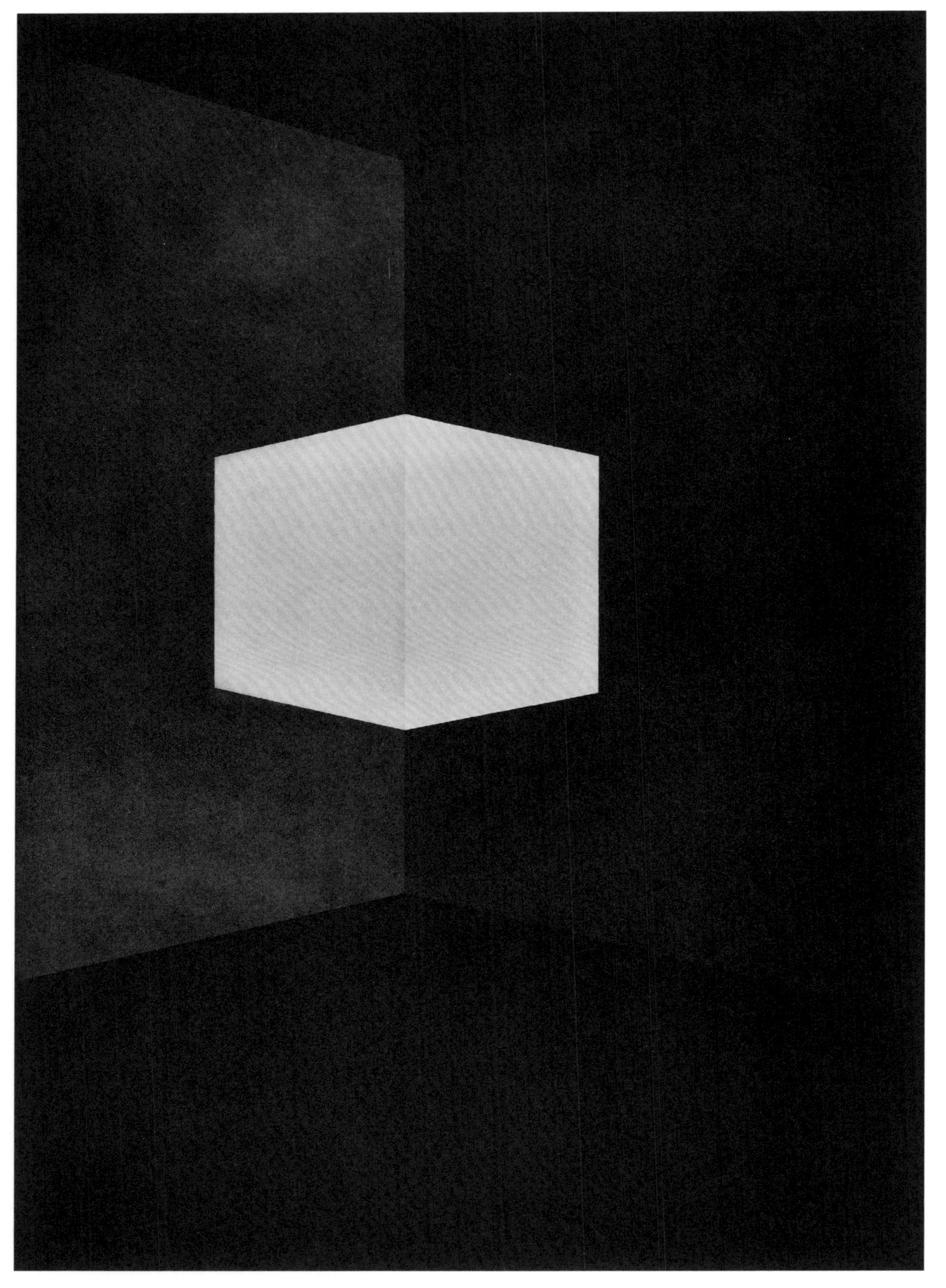

Afrum

Squat

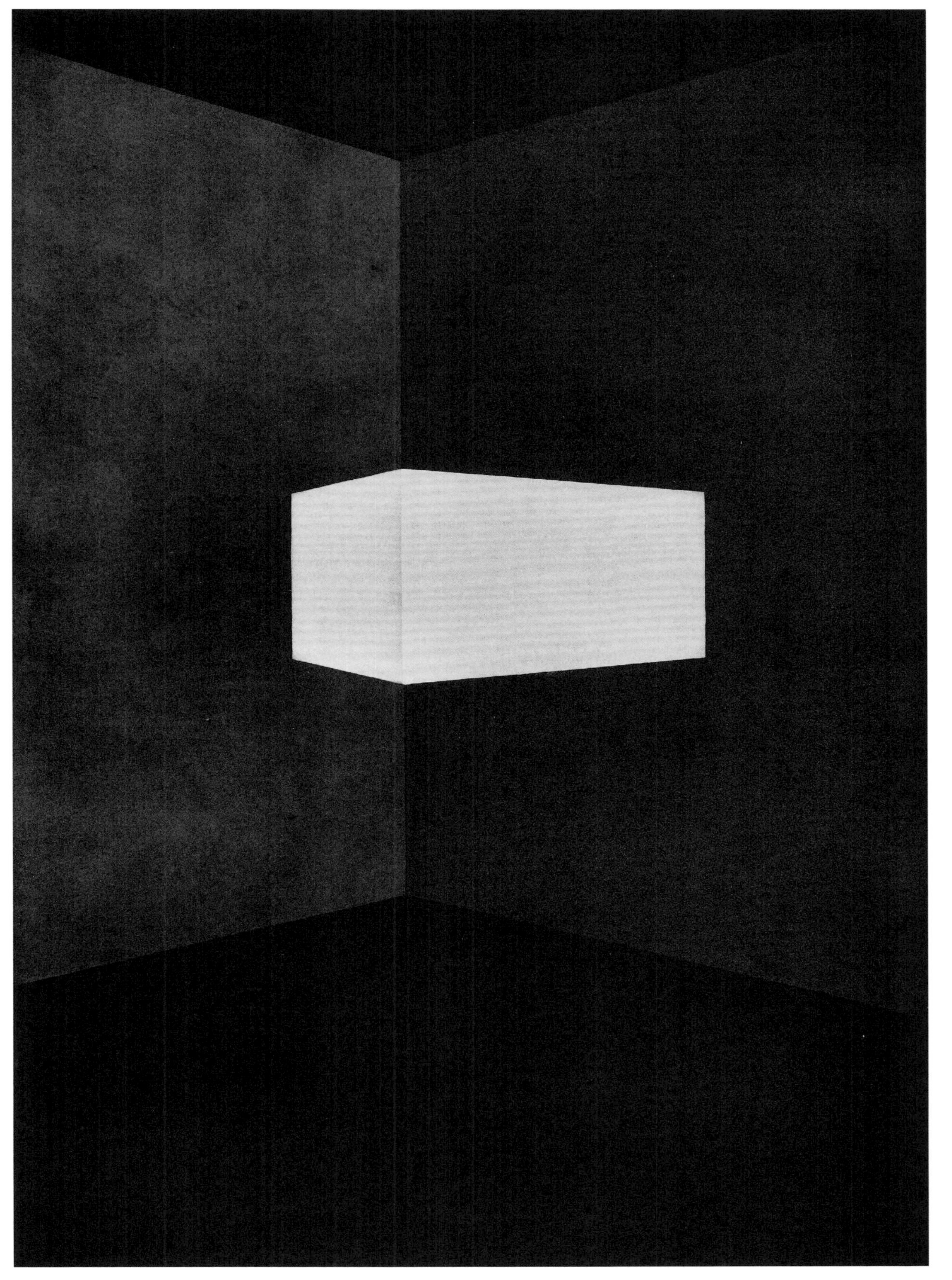

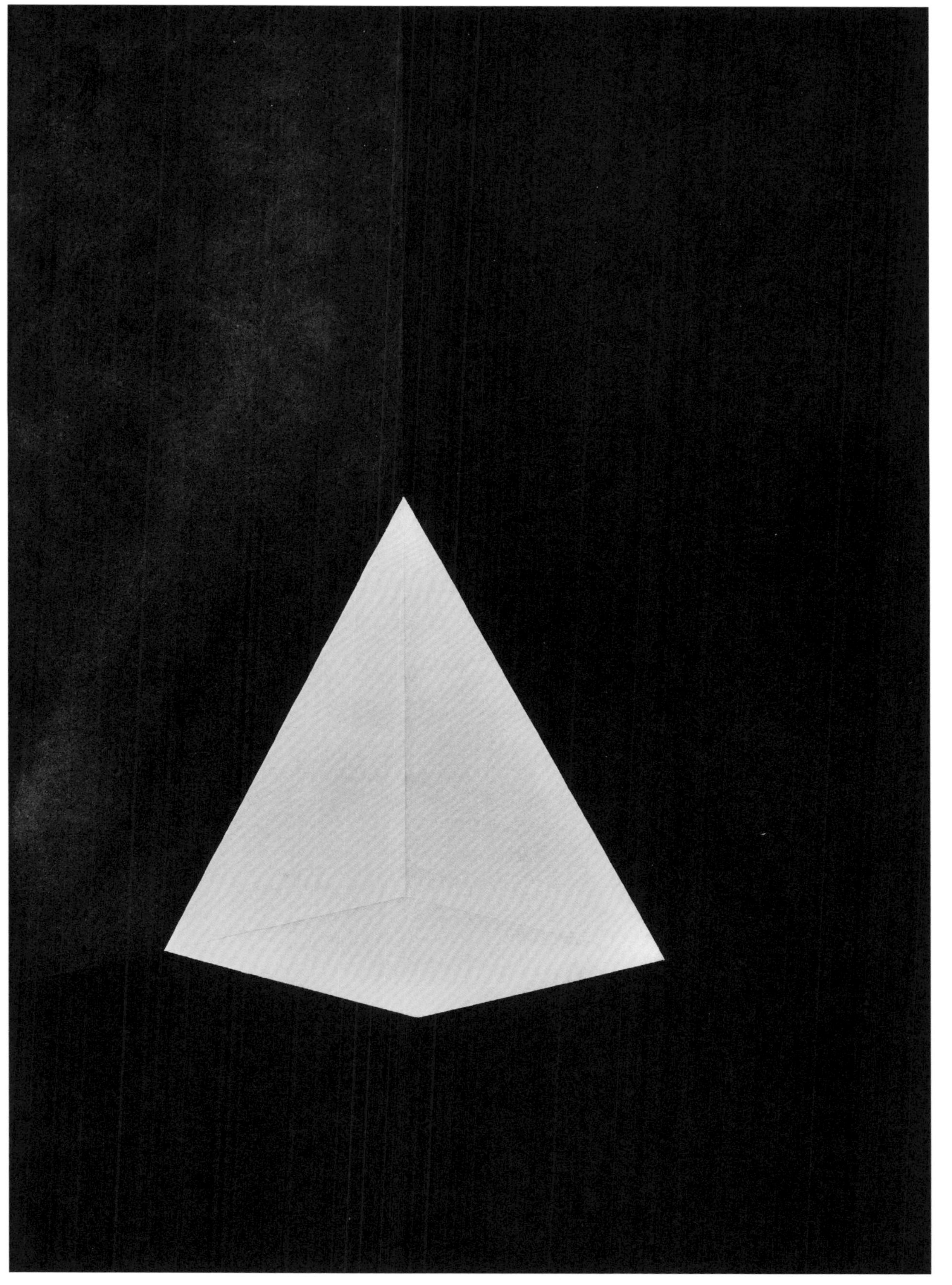

Mard

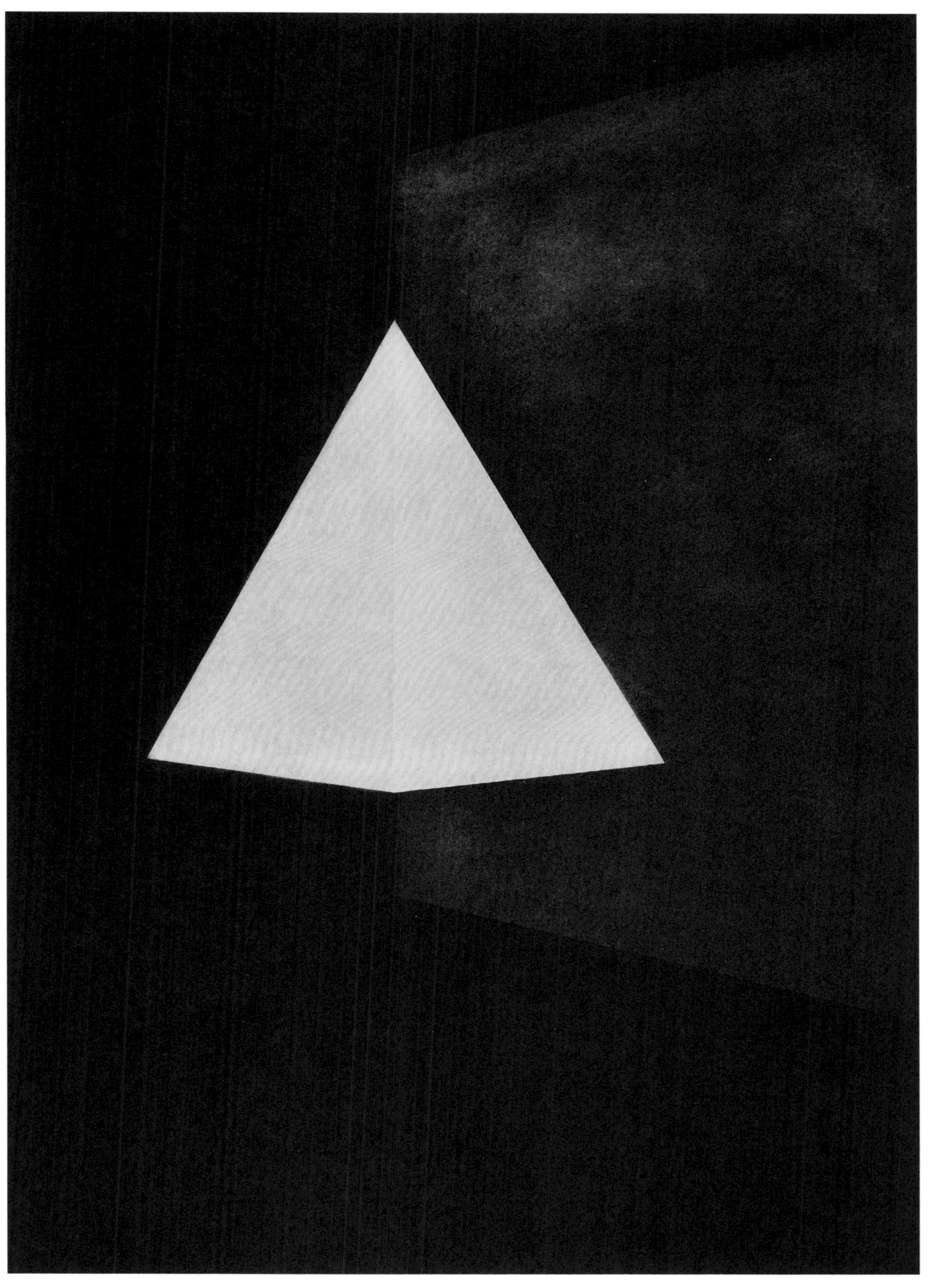

Raethro

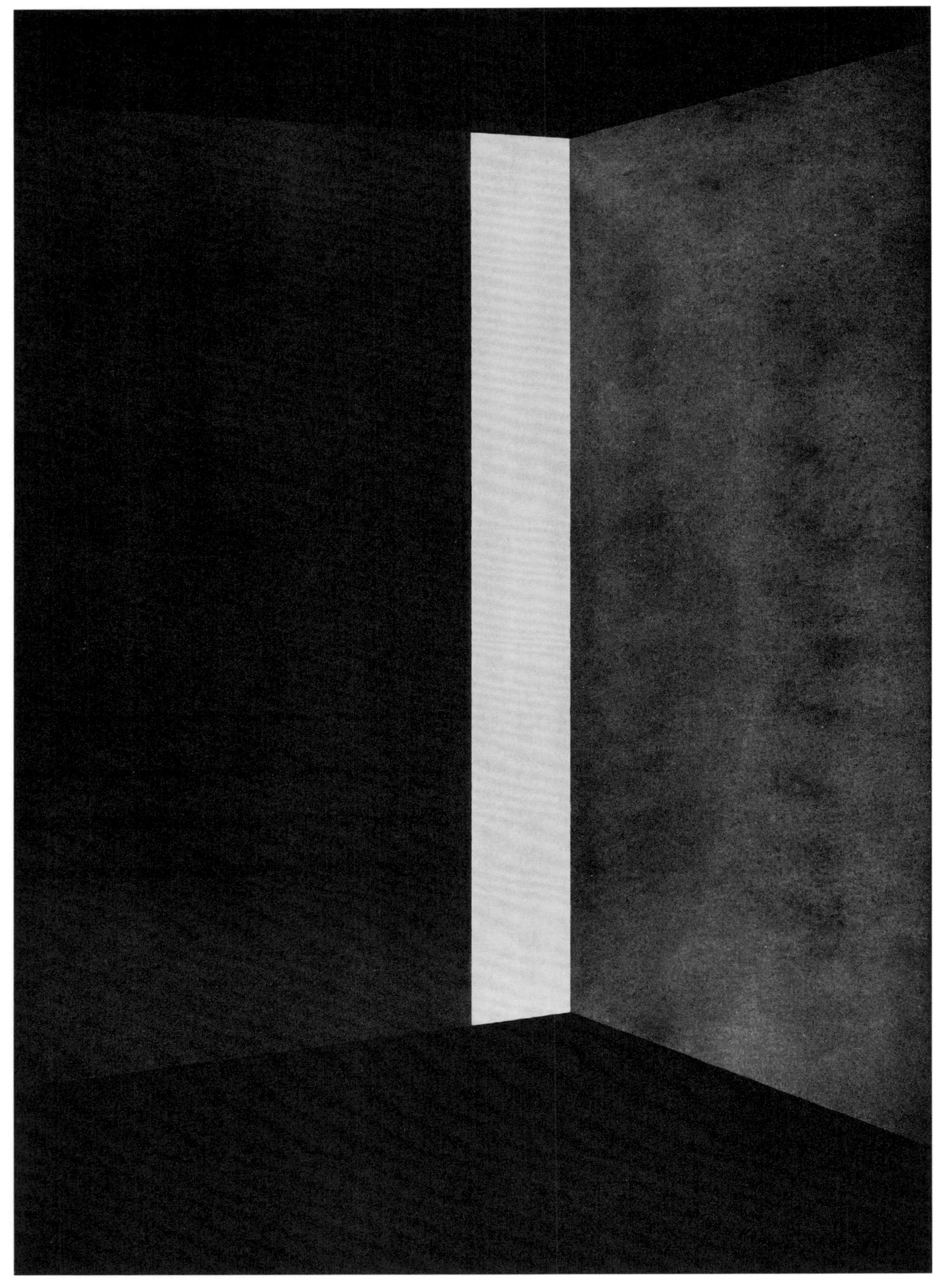

Tollyn

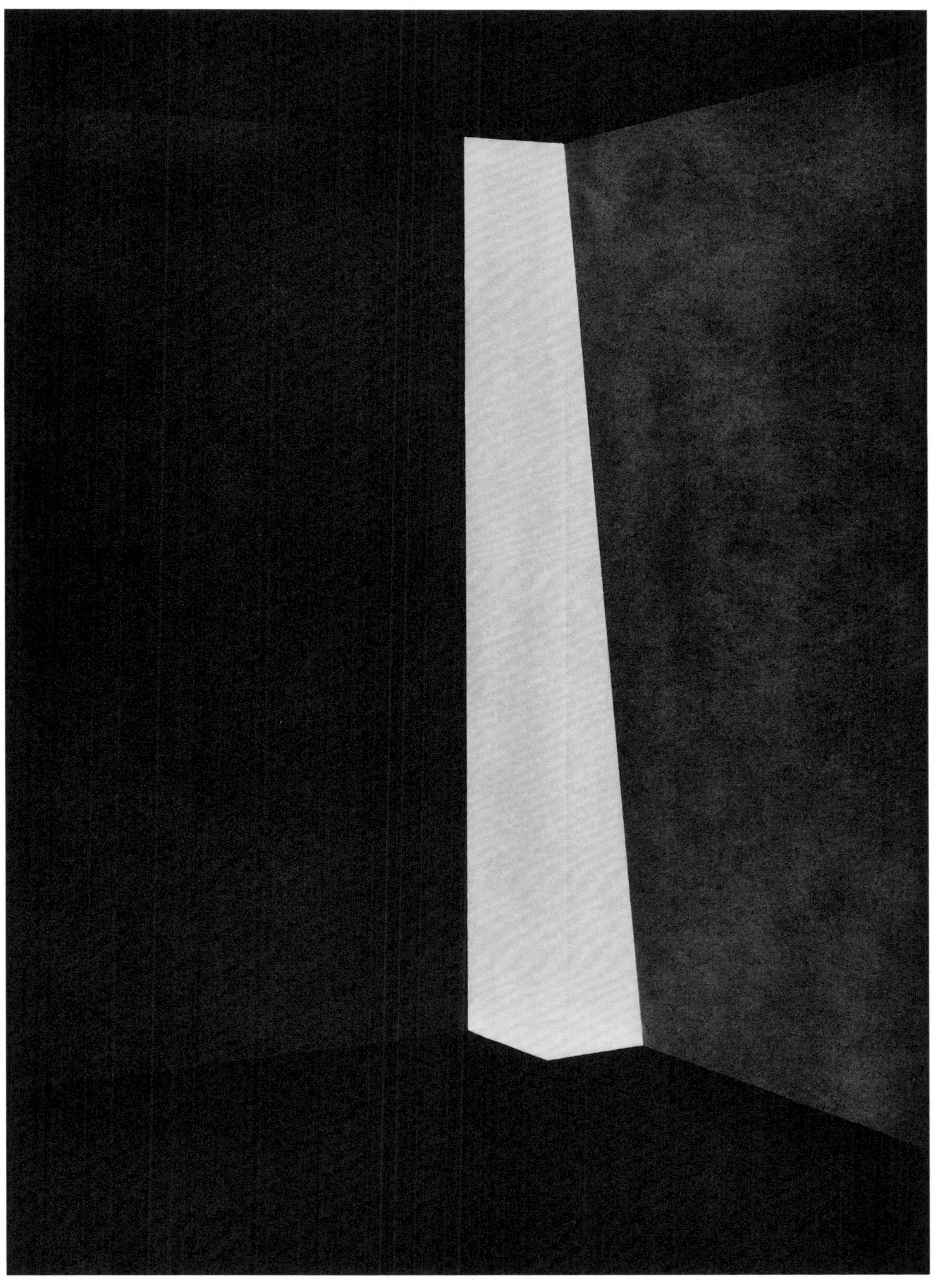

Enzu

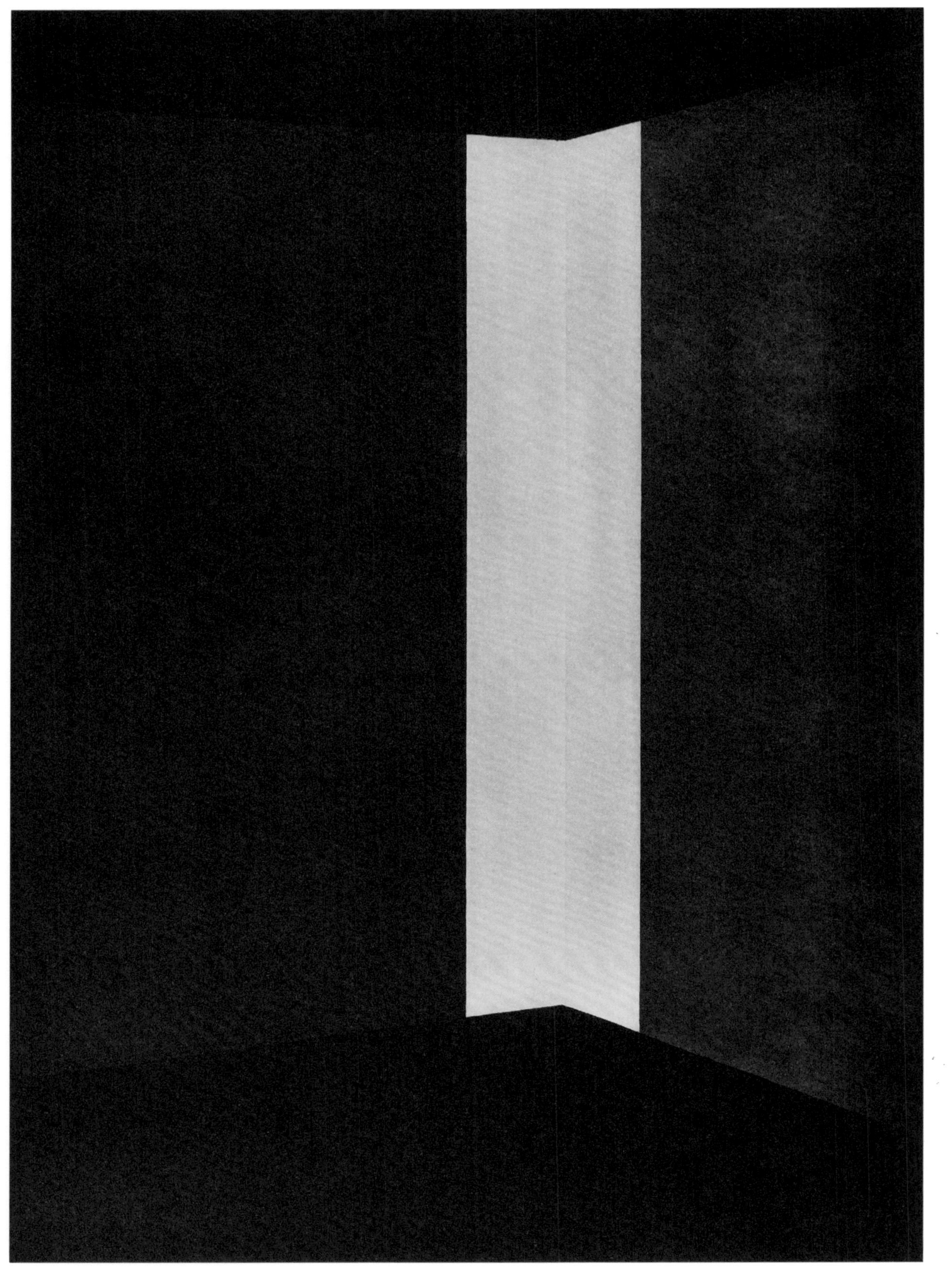

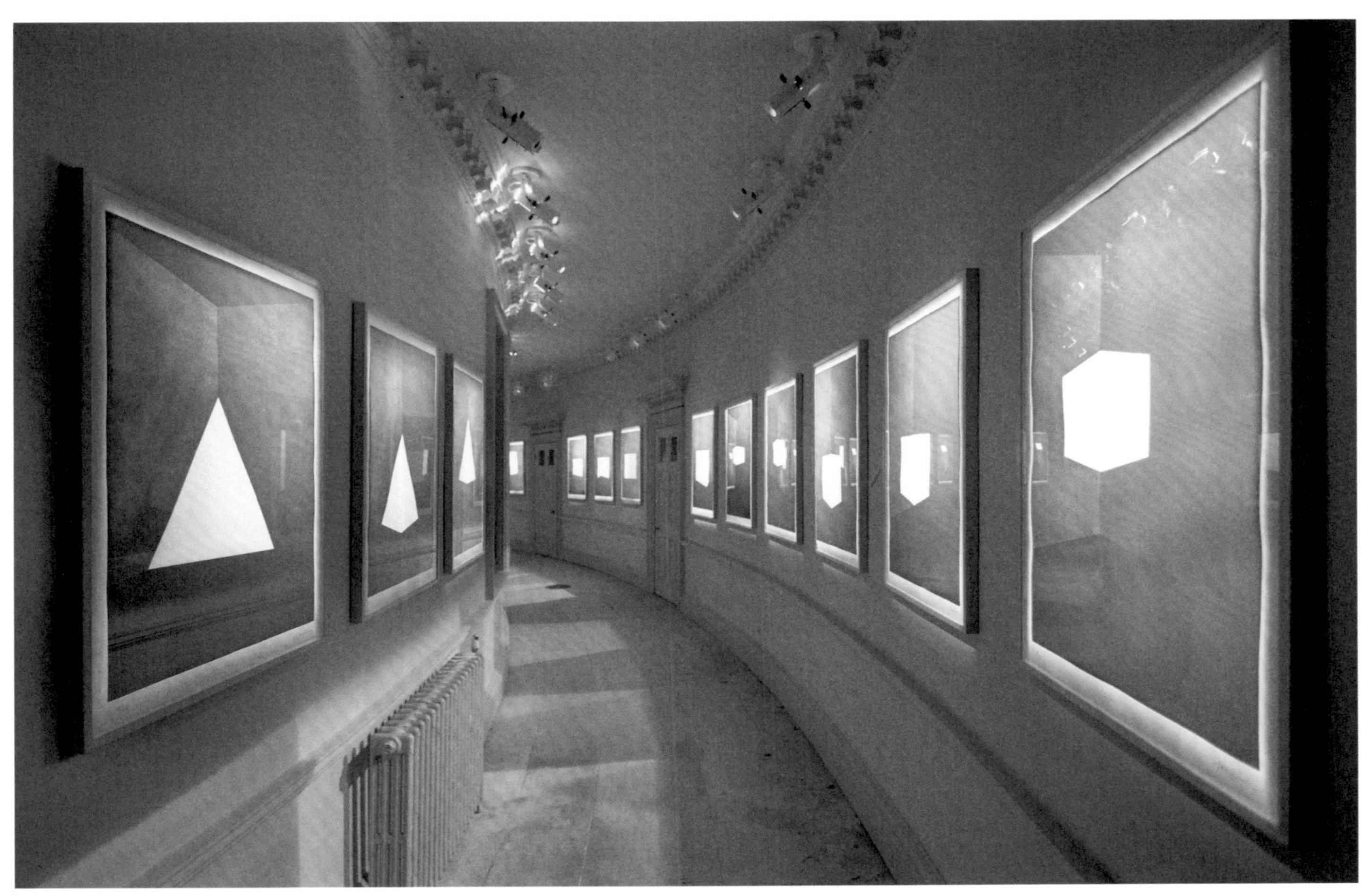

First Light, 1989–90, installed at Houghton Hall, North Colonnade, 2015

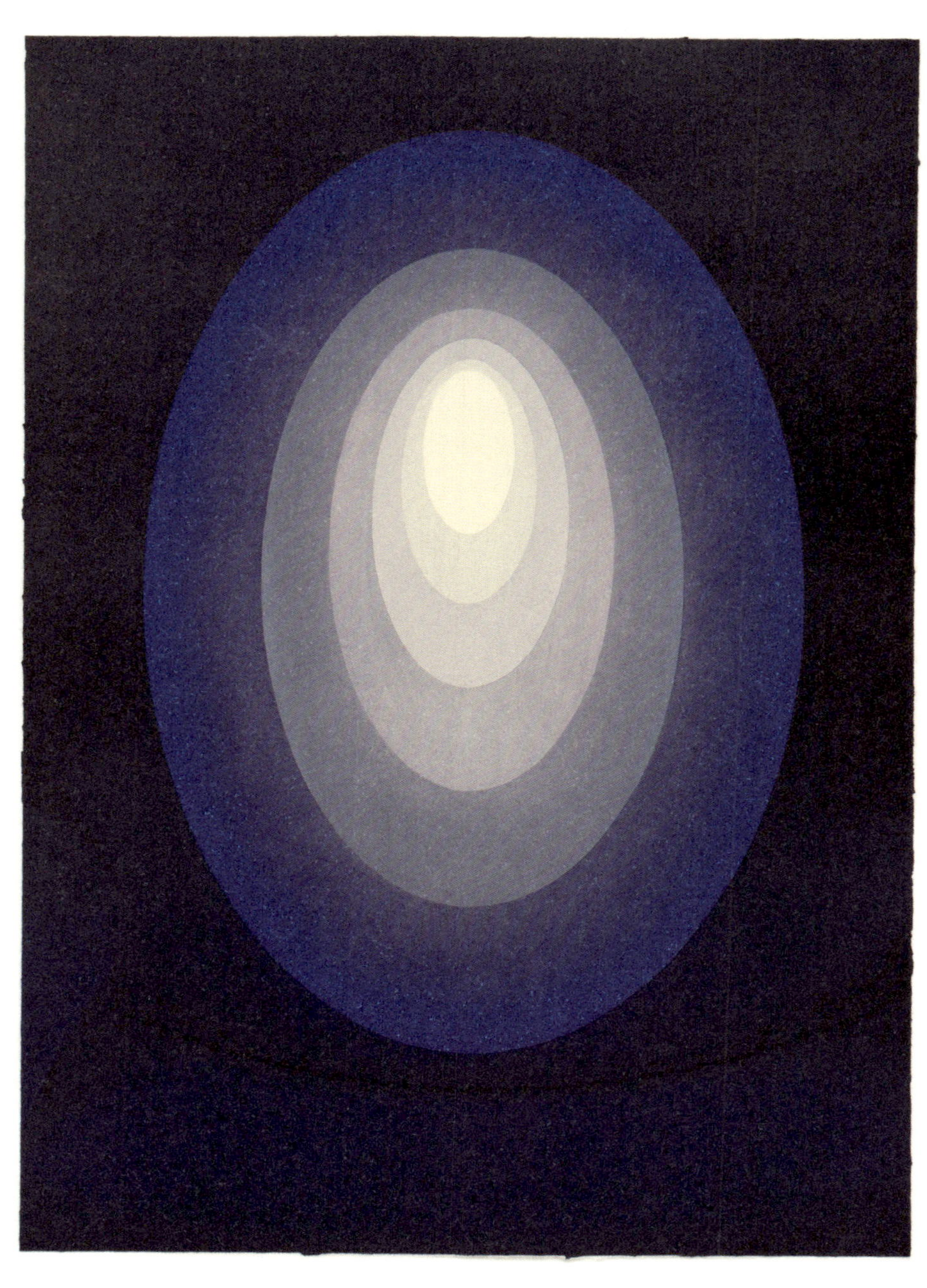

Aten Reign, from the Guggenheim, 2013

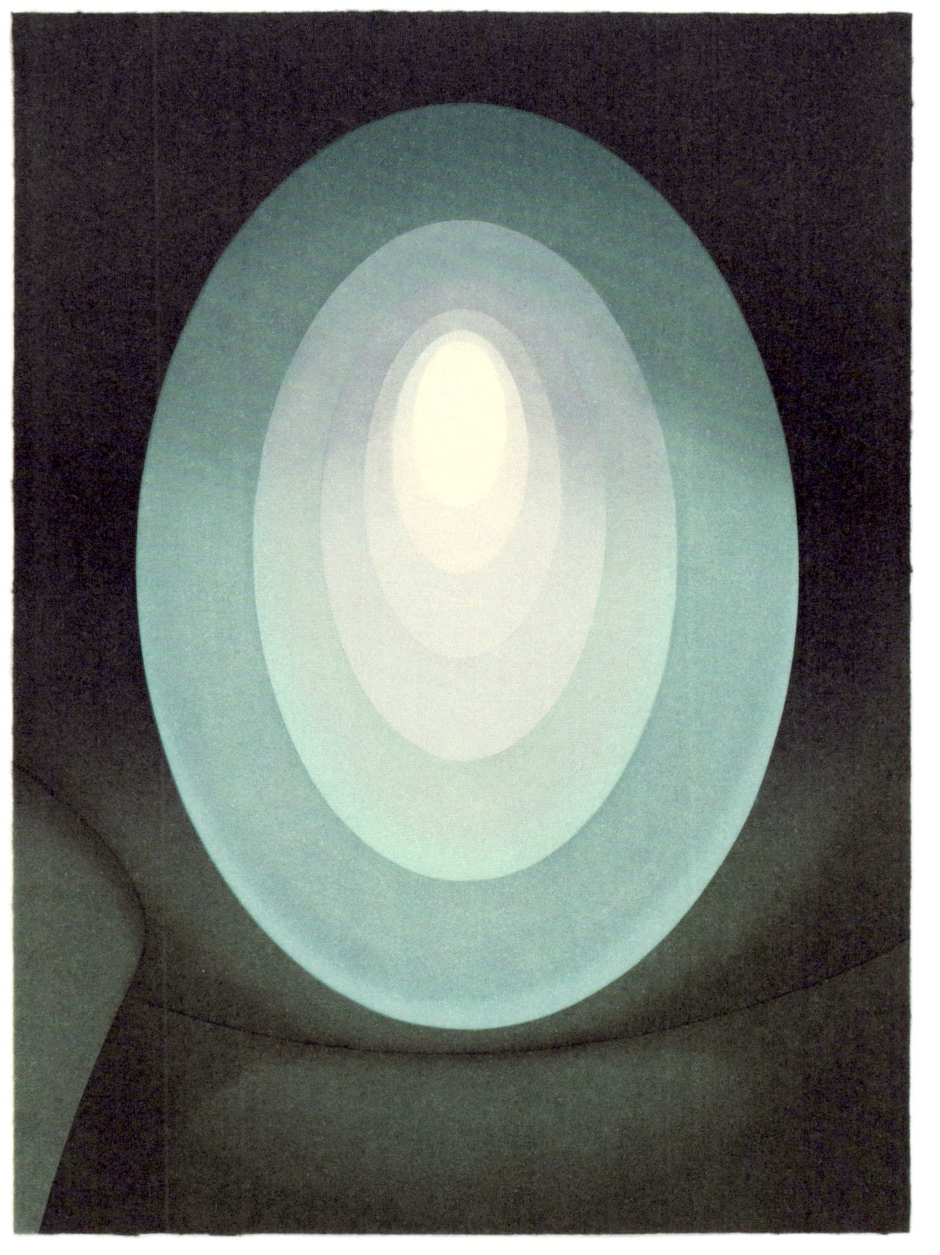

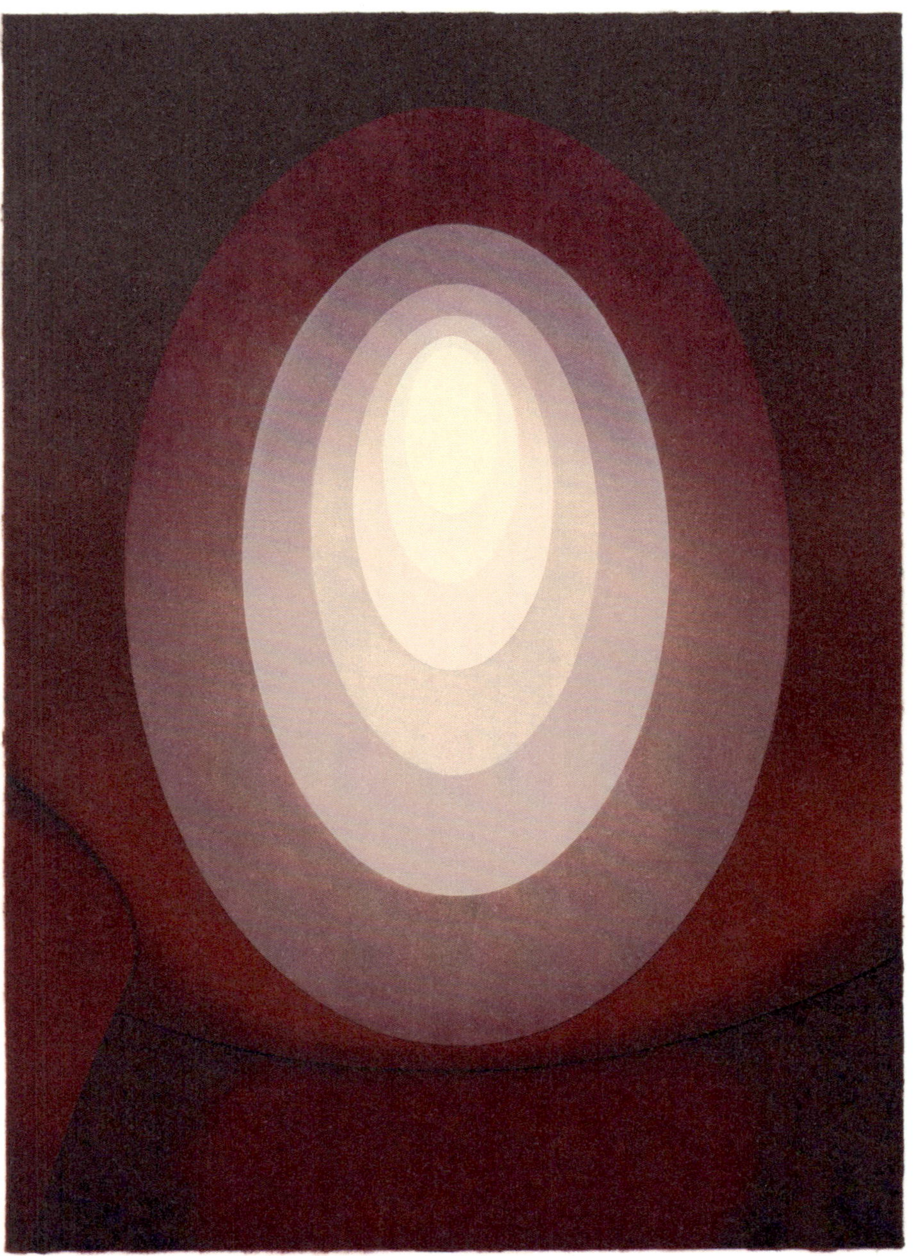

Exhibition List

pp. 23–31
Façade Illumination, Houghton Hall, 2015
Site-specific light installation

pp. 33–37
Seldom Seen, 2002
Skyspace

pp. 40–43
St. Elmo's Breath, 1992
Space division

p. 45
Raemar Magenta, 1970
Shallow Space
Courtesy the artist

p. 47
Raethro, Red, 1968
Projection piece

p. 49
Enzu, Green, 1968
Projection piece

pp. 51–53
Shirim, 2015
Tall glass, 183 × 123 cms

p. 55
Tortoise Beats Hare, 2015
Magnatron
Courtesy the artist

pp. 56–57
Untitled, 2010
Transmission hologram, blue ellipse, 158 × 112 cm / 62¼ × 44 in

pp. 58–59
Untitled, No. XXVG, 2008
Reflection hologram, orange triangle, 60 × 44.5 cm / 23⅔ × 44½ in

pp. 60–61
Untitled, No. XXX, 2012
Reflection hologram, green triangle, 61 × 43.2 cm / 24 × 17 in
Courtesy, Almine Rech Gallery

pp. 62–63
Untitled, No. XXVI, 2008
Reflection hologram, red vertical triangle, 61 × 33.5 cm / 24 × 13¼ in
Courtesy, Fundación Almine y Bernard Ruiz-Picasso para el Arte

p. 65
Roden Crater, 2010
Colour carbon print, 61 × 61 cm / 24 × 24 in
Courtesy the artist

p. 65
My First Roden Crater Photo, 2010
Colour carbon print, 61 × 101.5 cm / 24 × 40 in
Courtesy the artist

p. 67
East Portal, 2008
Plaster and bronze model, two halves, each 75 × 26.5 × 38 cm / 29½ × 10½ × 15 in
Courtesy, Häusler Contemporary, Munich

p. 68
Crater's Eye, 2008
Plaster and bronze model, two halves, each ∅52.5 × 12 cm / ∅17⅔ × 4¾ in
Courtesy, Häusler Contemporary, Munich

p. 69
South Space, 2008
Plaster and bronze model, two halves, each ∅45.2 × 12 cm / ∅17¾ × 4¾ in
Courtesy, Häusler Contemporary, Munich

pp. 73–92
First Light, 1989–90
20 Etchings in aquatint on Zerkall hand-made paper
each 113.5 × 80.5 cm / 44⅔ × 31⅔ in

pp. 94–95
Aten Reign, from the Guggenheim, 2013
Woodcuts on Tizutshi paper, each 67 × 47 cm / 26⅓ × 31½ in
Courtesy, the artist

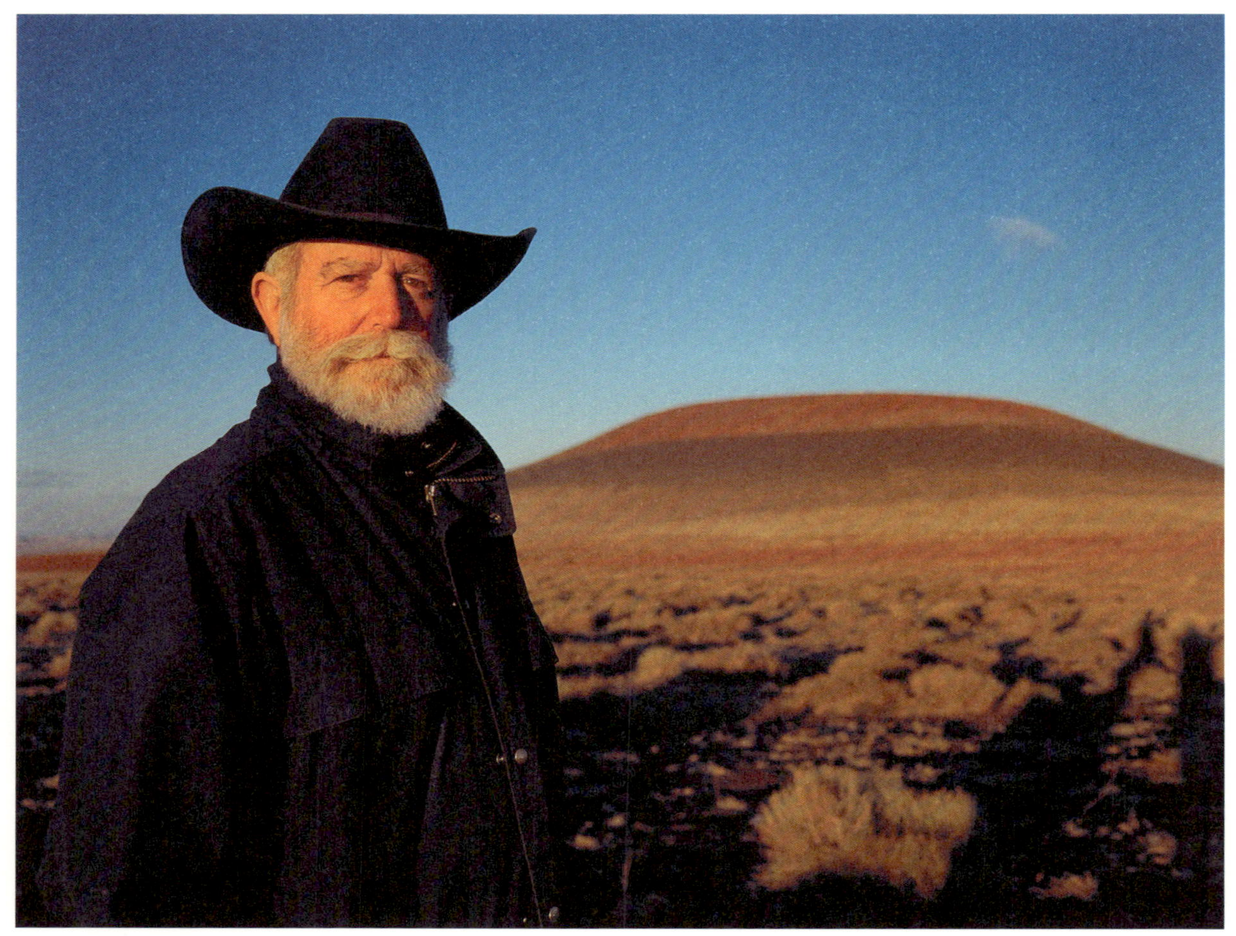

Photo: Florian Holzherr

James Turrell

6 May 1943, born in Los Angeles, California

1961, graduated Pasadena High School

1965, BA Psychology, Pomona College

1965–66, Art Graduate Studies, University of California, Irvine

1973, MA Art, Claremont Graduate School

AWARDS IN ART

1974, Guggenheim Fellowship

1984, Katherine T. and John D. MacArthur Foundation Fellowship

1991, Chevalier des Arts et des Lettres, France

1998, Wolf Foundation, Wolf Prize, Israel

2002, Honorary Fellowship, Royal Academy of Art, London, England

2004, Fellowship in the American Academy of Arts and Science

2006, Commandeur de L'Ordre des Arts et des Lettres

2011, National Academy of Arts and Letters

2011, American Academy of Arts and Letters

2013, National Medal of Arts

AWARDS IN ARCHITECTURE

2000, Grand Medailles d'Argent, Fondation Academie d'Architecture, Paris, France

2002, Jefferson Medal in Architecture, University of Virginia, Charlottesville, Virginia

2009, Fellow of the Royal Institute of British Architects, London, England

SELECTED SOLO EXHIBITIONS

1967
Pasadena Art Museum, California, *Jim Turrell*, 9 October to 9 November

1976
Stedelijk Museum, Amsterdam, Netherlands, *Jim Turrell: Light Projections and Light Spaces*, 9 April to 23 May
ARCO Center for Visual Art, Los Angeles, California, *James Turrell: Installation*, 16 November to 24 December

1980
Whitney Museum of American Art, New York, *James Turrell: Light and Space*, 22 October to 31 December

1983
Musée d'Art Moderne de la Ville de Paris, France, *James Turrell*, 20 December 1983 to 29 January 1984

1985
Museum of Contemporary Art, Los Angeles, California, *James Turrell: Occluded Front*, 13 November 1985 to 9 February 1986

1987
Kunsthalle, Basel, Switzerland, *James Turrell: Roden Crater Project und Licht-Raum*, 23 May to 5 July

1992
Henry Art Gallery, Seattle, Washington, *James Turrell Works 1967–1992*, 8 October 1992 to 3 January

1993
Hayward Gallery, Southbank Centre, London, England, *James Turrell: Air Mass*, 8 April to 27 June

1995
Art Tower Mito, Japan, *James Turrell*, 3 November 1995 to 28 January 1996.

1996
Stroom, The Hague, Netherlands, *James Turrell: Kijkduin*, 21 September 1996 to 20 March 1997

1997
Kunsthaus Bregenz, Austria, *James Turrell*, 27 July to 6 September

1998
Setagaya Museum, Tokyo, Japan, *James Turrell: Where does the Light in Our Dreams Come From?*, 13 August to 1 November
MAK, Vienna, Austria, *James Turrell: The Other Horizon*, 2 December 1998 to 21 March 1999

2000
Espace Electra, Paris, France, *James Turrell*, 26 April to 30 August

2001
Scottsdale Museum of Contemporary Art, Arizona, *James Turrell: Infinite Light*, 11 February to 9 September
Haus Konstruktiv, Zurich, Switzerland, *James Turrell*, 29 September 2001 to 11 April 2002

2002
Mattress Factory, Pittsburgh, Pennsylvania, *James Turrell: Into the Light*, 2 June 2002 to 30 April 2003

2003
Henry Art Gallery, Seattle, Washington, *James Turrell: Knowing Light*, 22 March 2003 to 8 February 2004

2004
IVAM, Valencia, Spain, *James Turrell*, 14 December 2004 to 27 February 2005

2005
Yorkshire Sculpture Park, Wakefield, England, *James Turrell: Light Installations*, 5 November 2005 to 14 May 2006

2009
Kunstmuseum Wolfsburg, Germany, *James Turrell: The Wolfsburg Project*, 24 October 2009 to 5 April 2010 (extended to 3 October 2010)

2011
Kulturhuset, Järna, Sweden, *See! Colour! James Turrell: The Light Inside*, 15 May to 2 October
Garage Center for Contemporary Culture, Moscow, Russia, *James Turrell*, 11 June to 21 August

2013
Los Angeles County Museum of Art, California, *James Turrell: A Retrospective*, 23 May 2013 to 6 April 2014
Museum of Fine Arts, Houston, Texas, *James Turrell: The Light Inside*, 9 June to 22 September
The Solomon R. Guggenheim Museum, New York, *James Turrell*, 21 June to 25 September

2014
Israel Museum, Jerusalem, *James Turrell: A Retrospective*, 1 June to 19 October
National Gallery of Australia, Canberra, *James Turrell: A Retrospective*, 13 December 2014 to 8 June 2015

SELECTED BIBLIOGRAPHY OF BOOKS AND EXHIBITION CATALOGUES

Adcock, Craig, *James Turrell*. Tallahassee: Florida State University Gallery and Museum, 1989

Adcock, Craig, *James Turrell: The Art of Light and Space*. Berkeley: University of California Press, 1990

Andrews, Richard and Chris Bruce, *James Turrell: Sensing Space*. Seattle: Henry Art Gallery Association, University of Washington, 1992

Butterfield, Jan, *The Art of Light and Space*. New York: Abbeville Press, 1993

Geometries of Light: The Roden Crater Project by James Turrell. Milan: Electra; Venice: University IUAV of Venezia, 2007

Graham-Dixon, Andrew and Clare Lilley, *James Turrell Deer Shelter: An Art Fund Commission*. London: The Art Fund, 2006

Haskell, Barbara and Melinda Wortz, *James Turrell: Light and Space*. New York: Whitney Museum of American Art, 1980

Häusler, Wolfgang, ed., *James Turrell: Lighting a Planet*. Ostfildern, Germany: Hatje Cantz, 2000

Herbert, Lynn M., John H. Lienhard, J. Pittman McGehee and Terence Riley, *James Turrell: Spirit and Light*. Houston: Contemporary Arts Museum, 1998

Holborn, Mark, *James Turrell: Air Mass*. London: South Bank Centre, 1993

Hue-Williams, Michael, *James Turrell: Eclipse*. London: Michael Hue-Williams Fine Art in association with Hatje Cantz, 1999

Hue-Williams, Michael and Andrew Graham-Dixon, with foreword by Louise T. Blouin MacBain, *James Turrell: A Life in Light*. Paris: Somogy Publishing, 2006

James Turrell. Bregenz, Austria: Kunsthaus, 1997

James Turrell. New York: Guggenheim Museum, 2013

James Turrell: A Retrospective. Los Angeles: Los Angeles County Museum of Art, 2014

James Turrell: Celestial Vault in the Dunes. The Hague: Stroom Den Hague Centre for Visual Arts, 1996

James Turrell: Infinite Light. Scottsdale, AZ: Scottsdale Museum of Contemporary Art, 2001

James Turrell: Into the Light. Introduced by Barbara Luderowski and Michael Olijnyk. Interview with the artist by Jim Lennox. Pittsburgh, PA: Mattress Factory, 2002

James Turrell: Light Spaces. San Francisco: Capp Street Project, 1984

James Turrell: Sensing Space. Text by Richard Andrews. Interviews by Richard Andrews and Chris Bruce. Seattle: Henry Art Gallery Association, University of Washington, 1992

James Turrell: Spirit and Light. Texts by Lynn M. Herbert, John H. Lienhard, J. Pittman McGehee, and Terence Riley. Houston: Contemporary Arts Museum, 1998

James Turrell: The Light Inside. Järna, Sweden: Kulturforum, 2012

James Turrell: The Other Horizon, Ostfildern, Germany: Hatje Cantz, 1999

James Turrell: The Wolfsburg Project. Ostfilden, Germany: Hatje Catz, 2009

Jim Turrell. Pasadena CA: Pasadena Art Museum, 1967

Jim Turrell: Light Projections and Light Spaces. Amsterdam: Stedelijk Museum, 1976

Rech, Almine, *Rencontres 9: James Turrell*. Paris: Almine Rech Editions, 2005

The Panza Collection. Texts by Giuseppe Panza and Evelyn C. Hankins. Washington, DC: Hirshhorn Museum and Sculpture Garden, Smithsonian Institution, 2008

ACKNOWLEDGEMENTS

David and Rose Cholmondeley, and the Trustees of Houghton, would like to thank the following for their help in planning and producing *LightScape*:

Sponsors Christie's and Pace Gallery, and members of the Foundation and Patrons Circles.

Lenders to the exhibition: Häusler Gallery, Almine Rech Gallery, Fundación Almine y Bernard Ruiz-Picasso para el Arte, James Turrell.

Kyung Lee Turrell, Ryan Pike, Julia Triebes, Tony Lee, Torsten Braun, Enliten Architectural Services Ltd, Bircham Electrical Ltd, Norfolk Drywall, PC Decorating Services Ltd, Westgreen Studio; Almine Ruiz-Picasso, Gwenvael Launey, Wolfgang Häusler, Mark Glimsher, Mollie Dent-Brocklehurst, Barry Diller, Ben Clark Charles Cator.

Peter Wilson and Jane Walsh of Theatre Royal Norwich; Robert Miller, Michael Morrison, Chris Bailey, John and Sheila Marchant, Dewynters, Bolton&Quinn, Johnny Cornwell, Andreas Siegfried, Martine d'Anglejan Chatillon, Stephen Murphy, Anna Bernardini, Alain Tarica, Pete Huggins, Peter Willberg, Linda Schofield, Peter Murray CBE, Hiram C. Butler, Florian Holzherr.

The house, building and administrative staff at Houghton.